EXPANDING
THE BORDERS
OF ZION

EXPANDING
the
BORDERS
of
ZION

A LATTER-DAY SAINT PERSPECTIVE ON LGBTQ INCLUSION

CHARLIE BIRD

EXPANDING THE BORDERS OF ZION: A LATTER-DAY SAINT
PERSPECTIVE ON LGBTQ INCLUSION | CHARLIE BIRD

The names included in this book may have been altered to maintain privacy.

ISBN 979-8-9869506-0-0 (Softcover)
ISBN 979-8-9869506-1-7 (eBook)
isbn 979-8-9869506-2-4 (Audiobook)

Printed in the United States of America
10 9 8 7 6 5 4 3 2 1

Book design by Firewire Publishing
Edited by Tracy Keck
Printed by Book Printers of Utah

Published by Birdhouse Book, operating under Charlie Bird Media LLC

DEDICATED TO RYAN & SHANNON
FOR FILLING MY LIFE WITH LOVE

CONTENTS

PREFACE

August 2022

SEVEN YEARS AGO, while on an international trip with my dad and younger siblings, we decided to take a long layover in Amsterdam to explore the city. I walked out from the central train station eager to see the meandering canals and gabled row houses that give the city its iconic seventeenth-century charm. My anticipation was met with disappointment, however, when I saw rainbow flags displayed on every corner. From signs posted along the main square I learned there had been a Pride celebration the day before. I was a recently returned missionary, and I clung to the hope that being gay was a choice. I viewed same-sex attraction as something to be overcome through righteous living, and thought anyone who identified as gay was weak, selfish, and sinful.

I walked around Amsterdam in disgust, keenly aware of each rainbow flag above my head. I felt awkward and uncomfortable, silently praying my family wouldn't recognize my distraction.

I hated every gay person in the world, and shuddered at the thought of a city that would glorify them. My internalized homophobia ran deep, and I associated Amsterdam's acceptance of LGBTQ people with litter in the streets. There was one alley in particular that was much dirtier than the rest, with trash covering its once-beautiful cobblestones. I believed if I ever accepted my orientation, the same contamination would happen to my soul. I captured a photo so I would never forget: gay = filth.

I had no idea what that belief would do to me in the coming years. No matter how hard I tried, I couldn't "get over" my orientation. I fasted, prayed, and yearned to be different, but nothing changed. Over time, my internal belief of "gay = filth" became synonymous with "Charlie = filth." I hated myself, and I felt increasingly distanced from God. My worldview was killing me from the inside out.

Thankfully, a lot has changed since then.

Through sincere effort and mighty prayer, I have developed a heathier and more accurate understanding of my orientation. While I once viewed it as a defect, I now view it as a gift. I know I was created intentionally by loving Heavenly Parents and that there is purpose in this part of my being. My orientation is not at odds with my identity as a child of God; both are a part of me. Accepting this truth has helped me become stronger, healthier, and closer to the Lord. It's helped me develop charity, gain Christlike empathy, and find unique ways to serve in God's kingdom. I wouldn't trade this part of me for anything—it has been the conduit through which I've exercised faith and come to know my Savior.

I recently went back to Amsterdam—as fate would have it, once again the day after a Pride parade. The city looked almost exactly as it had seven years ago, but I felt completely different.

When I saw filth in the streets, I didn't view it from a place of self-loathing and deem it a "consequence" for accepting LGBTQ individuals. I just viewed it as litter that was yet to be picked up. And when I saw historic buildings draped in rainbow colors, I didn't cringe with hatred and look away in disgust. Instead, I felt overwhelmingly grateful for how far I have come.

Seven years ago I thought I would always be alone in my struggle. But I was wrong. This time in Amsterdam, I walked the streets with three other young men, all of whom are also gay members of The Church of Jesus Christ of Latter-day Saints. Each of us, at some point in our lives, thought it was impossible to accept our orientations and still hold on to our beloved values and beliefs. But now each of us, in our own ways, are pioneering this trail.

It isn't easy. While we once faced the internal dilemma of reconciling our faith with our orientations, we now face the external complexity of membership in a Church where we don't exactly fit. At the intersection of faith and orientation, we exist at the apex of division. As we gather, worship, and serve, we are confronted with biases, misconceptions, and considerable pain. In many cases, it seems LGBTQ people at Church are expected to either hide who they are or find belonging elsewhere.

But is there really no place for God's LGBTQ children among believers?

I know so many people like me—children of God who identify as LGBTQ and hold fervent, sincere testimonies. We believe in the Restoration of the gospel, the power of the priesthood, and the importance of strong families. We desire the peace and hope found through Jesus Christ, and we want to exemplify Him in our words and deeds. We don't want to be feared or judged. We just want to live authentically, love fully, and not feel ashamed of who we are. We value service and we want to be full and active parts of every aspect of our communities, including coming to church to worship, regardless of orientation or relationship status.

We want to be there.

We want to belong.

But there are strong cultural currents that sometimes exclude us from Zion.

Throughout this book I will illustrate the blessings, challenges, and heartaches of being an LGBTQ member of the Church of Jesus Christ. Through personal stories, real-world examples, and gospel connections, I will highlight pain points, misconceptions, and cultural norms that drive God's LGBTQ children away and make it harder for us to feel welcome. I do this with the hope that you, the reader, will develop greater empathy and learn how to help the LGBTQ individuals in your sphere of influence feel more loved, wanted, and included. I pray you recognize your role and rise to the challenge. There is work to be done in this part of the vineyard.

There is work to be done in this part of the vineyard.

LGBTQ inclusion falls directly in line with gospel principles and counsel from modern-day prophets. Within the established doctrine of the Church of Jesus Christ, more space can be made for God's gay children. While I've worked hard to base my writing firmly in Gospel teachings, I recognize that some of what I've written may feel uncomfortable. As you read, I invite you to lean into discomfort and keep focus on our shared, most important

identities as covenant children of God and disciples of Christ.[1]
I trust the Holy Ghost to fulfill the role of Comforter and to
testify of truth (See John 14:16, Moroni 10:5).

Sharon Eubank once said, "This world isn't what I want it to
be. There are many things I want to influence and make better.
And frankly, there is a lot of opposition to what I hope for, and
sometimes I feel powerless."[2] I echo her sentiment when I consider how many priceless LGBTQ souls are failed by the membership of the Church. Too many have been lost to a damaging,
unchecked culture. It's easy to feel powerless and overwhelmed.
But walking through Amsterdam the second time gave me hope.
In just seven short years, my heart has transformed, and I have
become an unabashed advocate for healing and inclusion. If such
a powerful change can be borne in me, I have faith it can happen
in others, and in our religious community at large.

This is uncharted territory. When I wrote my first book on
this topic, *Without the Mask*, I felt very settled when it was
finished. The project was a hindsight look at my then-lived
experience, comprised of important lessons I had learned before
coming out. It was completely retrospective, and the final message felt complete, like a painting framed on a wall. This second
book feels much different to me, as if this painting is still in
progress. It doesn't just represent the journey I've had, but the
one I'm continually on. I'm sure as soon as this is published I'll
have new thoughts to add to the conversation and modifications
I wish I could make.

---

1   Russell M. Nelson, "Choices for Eternity," Worldwide Devotional for
     Young Adults, May 2022

2   Sharon Eubank, "By Union of Feeling We Obtain Power with God,"
     Ensign, November 2020.

It feels vulnerable to publish something so permanent when my life is such a work in progress, and I face continued scrutiny as a public figure in a very a polarized space. But even with the risks presented, I am proud of what I have written. I pray my words will heal hearts, mend families, and bring each person who reads them closer to Christ. My story is far from finished, but I trust God to lead me as I seek His counsel and move forward with faith.

If you are reading this as an LGBTQ or same-sex attracted person, I hope you know how important you are. I pray you feel the fullness of your divine worth. You are needed here, and I hope you will find the comfort and courage to worship God wherever you are in your journey. To the straight reader seeking to learn, I sincerely thank you for your willingness to enter this space. I know it might seem scary to seek proximity to the stories of LGBTQ individuals, but I invite you to open your heart and act in faith. I promise that by doing so, you will find God to be far greater than you have ever known.

EXPANDING THE BORDERS OF ZION

1.

BEYOND THE BARRIERS

THE COOL SEPTEMBER AIR was just beginning to change the leaves on the giant elm trees that lined "the mall" in Central Park. Tourists in light sweaters gathered in clumps, wielding selfie sticks and battling for the best view of street performers. My friend Jack was running late, so I spent a few minutes standing on a concrete blockade to watch some break dancers entertain while a crowd gasped in unison. The performers reminded me of my college days, entertaining crowds as the mascot at BYU. If I had been wearing different shoes I would have been tempted to join in.

Jack and I had made a habit of meeting in Central Park to share ideas, and, for lack of a better term, best practices. We had very similar backgrounds and were the only out, gay men in our small ward on Manhattan's East Side. Being an LGBTQ member of The Church of Jesus Christ of Latter-day Saints posed an array of spiritual and cultural challenges, but our ward was very accepting and embraced each of us without question. It made a

huge difference. Since we didn't have the usual social preoccupa-
tions that come with going to church while gay, we could explore
larger, more complicated questions concerning our experience.
Our ward's culture opened up a space where we could strive for
spiritual self-actualization, not merely social acceptance.

Jack showed up wearing a black sweater with baggy jeans.
His hair was cut short and he had a bag slung over his right
shoulder. We started catching up as we walked along a trail
through the park. He told me about his second year of law
school and the week he'd taken care of his brother's beagle. I
filled him in on my new job and a recent backpacking trip I'd
taken through Scotland. As we strolled beneath the tunnel and
across the terrace to the Bethesda fountain, our conversation
shifted from work and social updates to how we were navigating
our faith.

"I guess I don't really have much to report," I began. "Just
the regular issues—worrying I'll be lonely forever, feeling misunderstood, trying not to be jaded, and wondering where I fit
in God's plan. All very casual, you know?"

"You've never sounded less relatable," Jack said with a knowing laugh. "Tell me more."

He listened to my struggles the way only another gay member
of the Church could. We talked through my concerns, speculat-
ed about the future, and bonded over shared experience. Neither
of us had answers, but being with somebody who understood
helped me feel more at ease.

"Anyway, that's me," I concluded as we headed up the stairs
and past the cherry trees that lined the 72nd Street crossway.
"What's new with you?"

"Well, I started dating . . . ?"

"Whoa!" I stopped in my tracks. "What? Okay, back up. Tell me everything!"

Jack explained the thought process, emotions, and prayers that had led him to enter the unknown world of dating as a gay member of the Church. I was impressed with the mature way he was going about it. He'd talked to our bishop and had also been open with his family and a few close friends. As we walked along, he shared some of his positive dating experiences. He'd met interesting new people and discovered insights that had led to personal growth. We talked about the gift of agency, and how he'd felt God's love throughout the process. Jack also told me about the challenges he faced. He didn't have much experience maintaining personal boundaries and often felt judged for his morals and beliefs.

"Wow, that's a lot to figure out," I said as we sat on an empty bench.

"It is." He paused. "But honestly, there's something else entirely that's been weighing on my mind."

"What's that?" I asked.

"These guys I've been out with—they're all children of God."

"What an astute observation!" I said with a laugh.

"No, I'm serious!"

"Okay . . . ?" I ventured. "What's your point?"

"I guess I've always viewed other gay people as sinful and anti-religious. But as I've been with them, I'm realizing they're just like us. They all have divine heritage, and they're part of our heavenly family."

"I'm not really sure what you're getting at."

"So shouldn't we be sharing the gospel with them?"

"What?" I asked in disbelief. "Where did that come from?"

Jack told me about a man he'd been seeing named Omar. Omar was born and raised in New Jersey, but his parents were first-generation emigrants from Egypt, and he grew up practicing Islam. As Omar matured and realized he was gay, however, he couldn't see how his orientation fit within his parents' faith. Eventually, he let the religion slip away, along with any belief in God.

"So here's a man—" Jack continued, "—a son of God, almost thirty years old, who has no relationship with Deity and has never had the opportunity to learn about Christ."

"So you want to teach him the gospel?" I replied skeptically.

"Shouldn't he have that chance? What if he'd be interested?"

"I mean that all sounds wonderful . . . but, earth to Jack—he's *gay!*"

"So?"

"So . . ." I punctuated, "why would some random, agnostic gay guy ever want to come to *our* church?" Images of protests and Proposition 8 signs flashed through my head. More familiar images, of my younger self struggling to find a place where I fit, quickly followed.

"Why do you go?" he inquired.

"That's different."

"How?"

"Well, for starters, I was born into it."

"Okay. Why else?"

As I thought about my response, nostalgic images flooded my mind. First, I was eight years old, dressed in white, feeling the water glide over my face as I came up out of the baptismal font. Then I was eleven, silently praying in my closet, a Book of Mormon in my hand and tears streaming down my face. Memories of community, service, fun, and devotion kept coming, and I shared them aloud with Jack—kneeling in a circle to pray with my family, packing backpacks for refugees, dancing with friends to the electric slide, and reading a letter addressed to Elder Bird. So much of the growth and the beauty in my life had come because I was raised a member of the Church.

"You find value in it," he summarized.

"Yeah. I do." I replied, "If I didn't, I probably wouldn't be able to handle all the emotional turbulence."

"Exactly. So here *we* are, going every Sunday, keeping our covenants, and fighting to bridge the gap between our orientations and our faith. Who's to say Omar, or any other gay person for that matter, wouldn't want to do the same?"

I understood the point he was trying to make. If Jack and I found reason to attend church despite the hurt and confusion that membership presented us, maybe somebody else could find reason to come, too. But I still couldn't buy it. He was overlooking a glaring question: Why would any LGBTQ individual voluntarily waltz into the church that had caused us so much pain?

I thought about the years I had spent hating myself, and how they were informed by comments I'd heard at church. I remembered how I used to lie awake at night, haunted by the fear of being separated from my eternal family. I thought about each time I had fasted and prayed to be straight, and how heart-breakingly disappointed I was each time it didn't happen. For every positive memory I had growing up in the Church, there were at *least* two negatives.

Being a member of The Church of Jesus Christ of Latter-day Saints was more than religious affiliation. It was my culture, my identity, my home. And it wasn't always a welcoming home, or a safe culture. When I wasn't viewed in pity, I was viewed as a threat. It was exhausting to have a part of me that never fully fit in, no matter how hard I tried. And what, exactly, was the path for a gay member of the Church? No one seemed to know. Even with all my conviction, it was hard to hang on. Present understanding of gospel doctrine left many questions unanswered for gay Saints. There was enough uncertainty to last a lifetime, and I was haunted by eternal unknowns. How could I purposefully introduce that conflict into someone else's life? Was it setting them up for failure?

> **It was exhausting to have a part of me that never fully fit in, no matter how hard I tried.**

"So what's your plan, Jack? Invite gay people to church? Tell them it's great? Baptize them today and see if they have a disciplinary council tomorrow? Maybe we can make it work here in New York, but what happens if either of us move out of Manhattan? Do you think we'll be embraced by a new ward? It doesn't work that way—not when you're gay. How could you put that on someone else?"

"I get it, Charlie," Jack said seriously. "The Church has a *terrible* track record with the LGBTQ community. And I know exactly how hard it is to be a gay member. But this isn't just a problem in our church—it's happening everywhere."

He told me about a friend who was raised Presbyterian and grew up deeply devoted to his faith. In high school he went on missionary trips every summer and had plans to become a pastor. After he came out, however, things changed. He received pushback from leaders and was mocked by members of his congregation. In time, going to church felt dangerous to his mental, emotional, and spiritual health. He stepped away to protect himself and eventually renounced all of his beliefs. Like Omar, he never had the social support he needed to maintain his faith in God.

The story didn't surprise me—I knew it happened all the time. Churches push away gay people, so gay people push away faith. It was disheartening and tragic, but wasn't the same thing happening in our own religion? Most members of the Church I knew viewed gay people as outsiders, and treated them as such. How would inviting LGBTQ people to *our* church change anything? Jack's idea seemed crazy.

I voiced the thought.

"Because," he attested, "even though things are bad right now in our church too, I have faith in the gospel, and in its membership. We're not there yet. We're not even close. But I believe we have the tools to challenge these destructive social currents and become a refuge for God's LGBTQ children. I really think our congregations can become places where *all* are welcome to worship and come unto Christ, no matter their orientation."

"That's a beautiful belief, but I think you're living in the clouds. Too many people view it as us vs. them."

"Well, I'm not going to view it that way," Jack said firmly.

I opened my mouth to respond, then closed it again.

I thought about the LGBTQ people who were raised in my faith community. I knew the suicide rates. I saw the heartache, the loss, the confusion. I saw parents who disowned their children and individuals who felt forced into damaging life paths. It was heavy—so heavy—but I saw hope. I believed I could be an instrument for change, and that those who grew up in the Church could somehow find a way to reconcile longstanding beliefs with their identities. I believed if I tried hard enough, spoke loud enough, and wrote powerfully enough, I could carve out just enough space for people like me and Jack to keep going to church.

Because we were already part of the fold.

But LGBTQ people on the outside? No way. There was a marked line in the sand—a river—a *chasm* between gay people and The Church of Jesus Christ of Latter-day Saints. It was a rift I stared at every single day. It was the edge of the wilderness, off-limits, far beyond the charted boundaries. The barriers between my religion and the LGBTQ community had been established long before our time.

But Jack was looking beyond the barriers.

* * *

A few months later, Jack brought a man to church.

"Charlie, this is Omar," he said, a bright, gleaming grin on his face.

Omar wore a clean, pressed, checkered suit with a crisp white shirt and no tie. I welcomed him to the congregation and engaged in pleasant small talk, but in the back of my mind I wondered how things would play out. Our ward had been exceptionally supportive of Jack and me as single gay men, but would they offer that same acceptance to Jack and Omar as a couple?

But Jack's faith in our congregation was not misplaced. Everyone was helpful, welcoming, and bright. When the bishop walked by, Jack waved him over and gave Omar a glowing introduction. They hit it off quickly, talking about work, travel, and what subway lines Omar took for his commute. Just before the top of the hour, the bishop went up to the stand and the three of us took seats on the middle row with a group of friends.

Julie and Savannah, who had met Omar before, helped explain the general proceedings and what to expect during the sacrament. When the opening hymn began, Carly, the Relief Society president, shared her hymnbook with Omar.

The meeting was beautiful—one of the best I'd ever been to. The speakers were clear, concise, and focused on core gospel doctrines. Omar listened intently, taking in his first messages of faith, repentance, and Christ's redeeming love. Later, during the elders quorum lesson, he sat on the front row, asking thoughtful questions and taking notes on an iPad. His presence made everyone more attentive and engaged. We didn't take turns reading line by line through the lesson manual as per usual. Instead, we bore our testimonies, cross-referenced scriptures, and shared experiences that fostered riveting discussion.

The following night I met up with Jack to get the full scoop. I was dying to know what Omar thought about church and what kind of conversation they'd had on the way home. I learned that Omar had really liked it and expressed interest in coming again. He felt welcomed and comfortable and enjoyed learning more about the religion Jack was so fond of. After church they'd talked with the missionaries, and to my surprise, Omar had scheduled a lesson with them later in the week.

I was impressed with Omar, and with Jack's bold move to invite him to church, but I still felt the whole thing was a little far-fetched.

"So, what do you expect?" I asked about halfway into dinner. "You're hoping to what, baptize your boyfriend?" I said with a laugh.

"Only if he wants to."

"You can't be serious!" I countered.

"I'm not really expecting anything. I just want Omar to choose what's best for him. All I know now is that I liked having him there. And he liked it too."

All I could see were problems . . . the policies, the people, the past . . . I could think of about a million, but I didn't list any of them out loud.

"He's reading the Book of Mormon," Jack said.

"Really?" I questioned in surprise.

"He asked me for a copy last night. He's already in Second Nephi."

"That's amazing!" I responded.

"I know," Jack agreed.

We sat in silence for a bit.

"Look, like I said," he continued, "I don't really know where this is going. Maybe it won't go anywhere. But I do know that I care about Omar, and God cares about him too. I want him to have the same knowledge and opportunities I have. I want him to be able to add to his existing faith, and understand me more through learning about what I believe. Will he get baptized? Probably not. But still, couldn't coming to church, reading the scriptures, and associating with our beliefs be meaningful to him? Couldn't it add value to his life? Couldn't it help him develop faith and build a relationship with Christ?"

"Who knows?" Jack continued. "Maybe God put Omar in my path for a reason."

On the way home I thought more about Jack's question as to why I hadn't left the Church. He was right. I did find value in it, and I always had. But it was more than that—I believed it. I had sincere love for the restored gospel of Jesus Christ. My testimony was based in deep-rooted conviction of truths I couldn't deny.

I'd seen miracles, made meaningful covenants, and felt the Spirit illuminate my heart time and time again.

Being a gay member of the Church was difficult and often disappointing, but to me it was still worth it. If I felt I could explore Christ's teachings and gather with the Saints, no matter what my life looked like, why wouldn't I give that same opportunity to others? Why would I maintain a barrier regarding who could come unto Christ?

> ## Why would I maintain a barrier regarding who could come unto Christ?

The Book of Mormon contains powerful stories about how removing such barriers can expand the borders of Zion. Missionary efforts in scripture almost always start with someone courageously choosing to act in love. Alma the Younger and the sons of Mosiah are fantastic examples of this. Ammon, especially, showed courage and character beyond compare. In Alma 26, we learn that when Ammon and his brothers first decided to go live among the Lamanites, they were laughed to scorn. The majority of the Nephites thought the idea of associating with the Lamanites was absurd, and they wanted to "take up arms against them" and fight (v. 25). Even against all this backlash, Ammon and his brethren gave up the chance to rule the land of Nephi and instead embarked on the dangerous, seemingly impossible task of integrating with the Lamanites. Even though people thought he was crazy, Ammon did what he knew was right anyway.

When Ammon arrived in the land of Ishmael, he was taken and bound. Due to the complicated past between their tribal groups, the Lamanites didn't trust him. They had incredibly different cultures and an ugly history of war, violence, hatred, and miscommunication. When Ammon was brought before King Lamoni to be questioned, the king asked "if it [was Ammon's] desire to dwell in the land among the Lamanites." Ammon confidently responded, "Yea, I desire to dwell among this people for a time; yea, and perhaps until the day I die" (Alma 17:22–23).

Imagine the faith and cultural humility this response would require. Ammon chose to dedicate his whole life to serving the Lamanites according to their own customs. He didn't preach to them or implore them to change. Instead, he got out of his comfort zone and served. When King Lamoni's flocks were threatened by robbers, Ammon risked his own safety to defend them. When asked about his beliefs, Ammon used familiar terms and met the king right where he was. When the queen was distraught and asked for guidance, he sat with her and offered comfort.

His approach brought miracles. Ammon's humble service led to one of the greatest missionary success stories in the Book of Mormon, and converted an entire nation, bringing tens of thousands to the knowledge of their Redeemer. It mended broken ties between the Nephites and the Lamanites and led to increased peace in the land. Both groups were able to learn from one another, and many souls were enlarged through new associations with long-lost kindred.

Ammon chose *connection* instead of correction. Even though the Lamanites were different than himself, he moved in. He got closer. He learned from them and served them. He threw out his discomfort, including every preconceived notion he had, and strived to see each individual as an equal and a beloved child of God. He gave his time, talents, and efforts, expecting nothing in return. When they were attacked, he defended them. When they were low, he comforted them. He saw their divine potential and honored their existing faith.

Ammon chose connection instead of correction.

We follow Ammon's example when we do the same.

* * *

As covenant people of the Lord, we are commanded to overcome division and expand the borders of Zion. Doctrine and Covenants 82:14 says, "For Zion must increase in beauty, and in holiness; her borders must be enlarged; her stakes must be strengthened." Part of enlarging Zion's borders and strengthening her stakes means diversifying who feels comfortable worshipping with us. We increase in beauty as we know and learn from one another, and we gather Israel by expanding our circles of love. As the scriptures teach, "[God] inviteth them all to come unto him and partake of his goodness; and he denieth none that come unto him, black and white, bond and free, male and female; and he remembereth the heathen; and all are alike unto God" (2 Nephi 26:33).

There is a common assumption, held by Christians and LGBTQ people alike, that gay people don't belong in churches. This mentality has led to division and dissension all over the world and has amplified stereotypes, biases, misconceptions, and fears. But hope is not lost, because barriers can be removed. As covenant members of The Church of Jesus Christ of Latter-day Saints, we can challenge that assumption. We can reach out to others in love, driven by our core belief that *all* are children of

God. We can honor the divinity in our friends and neighbors and strive to make space for each of them. Our congregations can be numbered among the safest, most welcoming places for God's LGBTQ children and can be environments where everyone can develop and maintain strong, secure faith in Him.

I know it's possible, for I've witnessed it firsthand.

When I reflect on the time I spent in the Manhattan YSA Ward, the memories aren't complete without Jack and Omar in the sixth row, wearing matching red-striped Dockers. They were a staple to the ward, exemplifying powerful, persistent faith. Omar read the entire Book of Mormon twice and regularly met with missionaries. He hosted watch parties for general conference, visited with the bishop often, and befriended newcomers to the congregation.

Because he wasn't an official member, Omar couldn't receive a calling, but he requested an assignment to clean the church, happy to scrub toilets if it meant he could serve. Every Saturday morning he woke up early, took a train across town, and met Jack at the meetinghouse to vacuum the floors, clean the bathrooms, and wash the windows. His church participation wasn't just born out of love for Jack, but from his own dedication. On weeks when travel, work, or other circumstances prevented Jack from attending church, Omar showed up to sacrament meeting alone. Involvement in our ward gave him community and belonging, and a place where he could develop a meaningful relationship with God.

Four years later, Jack and Omar are still together and attend church as a couple each week. They are now in a different ward, where they again enjoy a strong sense of acceptance and belonging. They continue to seek opportunities to serve and find value in gathering with the Saints. Omar has not been baptized, but he feels grateful for his association with the Church and how it has helped him find God. Even though Jack and Omar are not "typical" members, everyone I know is better for knowing them. Their relationship has blessed many lives, including my own.

I have a sincere testimony that God loves His LGBTQ children. We are sent to earth for a divine purpose, and we are integral members of our heavenly family. We are so much more than the stereotypes that surround us. When given the opportunity, we are lights to our wards and communities. The worth of LGBTQ souls is great, and we need everyone included if we truly are to establish Zion. Let us move beyond any barrier that would keep us from doing so.

We need everyone included if we truly are to establish Zion.

May we overcome the us vs. them mentality that divides us.
May we heal from the wounds of our past.
May we extend belonging to all of God's children.
May we expand the borders of Zion.

2.

THE LOST CHAROLAIS

OR ME AND MY OLDER SISTERS, childhood chores usually revolved around cattle. Most of my early memories consist of stacking hay bales, bottle-feeding calves, and shoveling manure out of a forty-three-foot gooseneck trailer. On my favorite days, I got to ride on the back of the truck and count the cows in each pasture. I loved holding on to the steel tread of the flatbed while my dad drove slowly through the field. From up there I had the best vantage point to make sure each cow was safe and accounted for.

I always kept a keen eye out for my favorite one. I could easily recognize her by her light Charolais color and her larger-than-life eyes. We all laughed the first time we saw the cow. Her lashes were at least two inches long, and she had gray-blue eyelids that made her look like she was wearing makeup from an '80s music video. I talked about the "makeup cow" so much that my dad eventually gave her to me.

One day as I was counting, my heart sunk to my stomach. After multiple scans of the pasture, my cow's smoky blue eyes were nowhere in sight. I tapped on the cab until the truck came to a gentle stop, then I hopped off the back and broke the news to my dad and sisters. They could see how worried I was, and we all immediately set out to look for my lost cow.

We searched the pasture and eventually found a gap in the barbed-wire fence that lined the perimeter. To my dismay, there were disruptions in the tall grass indicating that my favorite cow had indeed made it through the fence and was gone. Her trail was quickly lost among brush and tight-packed trees that covered hundreds of acres of untouched state conservation land.

We decided to spread out to cover more ground. Walking about twenty meters away from each other, we carefully climbed through the fence and began bushwhacking into the unknown. We spent what felt like forever trudging through the undergrowth and tripping over rocks. Spiderwebs caught my face and roots pulled at my feet as we marched along. Occasionally the trees would open up, seemingly offering a break from the madness, but thistles, thorns, and briars attacked me on every front. The hot sun beat down, causing sweat to form on my neck and brow, attracting bugs, dust, and pollen. A few times I feared that *I* might get lost before we ever found my cow. I had to call out to my dad and sisters to make sure we were all within range of each other.

Eventually, after about a mile of misery, we found her at an opening near a river that passed through the land. She looked relieved, and blinked at us with her big, long lashes. Apart from a few briars and scratches, she looked as beautiful as ever, and I was happy to see her in good shape. We circled around and slowly made the long return trek through the wild, ushering her back to the pasture where she belonged. Once there, she joined the herd and we worked to repair the hole in the fence.

Later that evening, when I finally made it home to shower and get cleaned up, I found ticks crawling all over my body. I had bug bites from both mosquitos and chiggers, proving miserable through the night. The next morning I woke up with a poison ivy rash all over both of my legs. I decided that searching through the brush for lost cows was officially my least favorite thing in the world, but deep down I knew I would do it again if I had to. The satisfaction of finding my cow and leading her home was worth every discomfort. I could rest easy knowing she was safe and sound, back in the pasture where she belonged.

In Matthew 18, Christ recounts the parable of the lost sheep. He said, "How think ye? if a man have an hundred sheep, and one of them be gone astray, doth he not leave the ninety and nine, and goeth into the mountains, and seeketh that which is gone astray? And if so be that he find it, verily I say unto you, he rejoiceth more of that *sheep,* than of the ninety and nine which went not astray" (vv. 12–13).

In most depictions I've seen of this parable, the Savior is featured with a lamb over His shoulders, walking on a beautiful mountain path to return the lost sheep back home to the fold. There's usually a sunset sky in the background with pleasant, inviting colors. While I love a good Christ-centered landscape painting, I feel like going out to find lost sheep isn't always such a sunset stroll in the mountains. In fact, I imagine it feels a lot more like searching for a lost cow on Missouri conservation land. In order to find those who are lost and bring them back to the fold, we have to push through undergrowth and get tripped up by roots. We have to bushwhack through the wilderness, and worry whether we might be lost. Then, the next morning, we might even have to deal with the aftermath of bug bites and poison ivy.

It takes concerted spiritual and emotional effort to seek out and find lost sheep. We can't expect to sit back in the field with the ninety and nine and end up accidentally establishing Zion. Sometimes we have to crawl through the fence and get ourselves dirty.

In the parable of the wheat and the tares, the Savior taught that we are to be gatherers, not sifters. He illustrated that it's not our job to think about whether someone is a wheat or a tare. Instead, we are called to gather all of God's children into the harvest. I used to think sharing the gospel only meant setting my righteous life on a hill to be seen. I imagined others would see my light and flock to it, eager to have the happiness and peace I experience as a faithful Latter-day Saint. I now realize gathering Israel takes much more than that. Christ's work is done in the margins. Rather than wait for people to come to us, we must shake ourselves from our comfort and go to them. In a way, we have to scatter ourselves in order to gather. We have to move beyond any barriers and interact with all kinds of people—to spread out and cover more ground. We must connect with people from different religions, cultures, ethnicities, and backgrounds, and include LGBTQ individuals in our view of Zion.

> ## It's not our job to think about whether someone is a wheat or a tare.

President Russell M. Nelson has counseled the Lord's covenant people to "expand our circle of love to embrace the whole human family."[3] He also taught that "the gospel net to gather scattered Israel is expansive."[4] With this in mind, I no longer view the gathering of Israel as bringing others into the small circle of Zion. Instead, I view it as expanding the borders of Zion to ensure it encompasses each one of God's children. We establish Zion as we seek to know one another's hearts. We expand Zion's borders when we erase the boundaries of who we choose to love.

Part of seeking to know one another's hearts means putting off our own preconceived notions. As covenant members of Christ's Church, we have a duty to overcome and correct outdated cultural beliefs regarding race, gender, and orientation that inhibit us from establishing Zion. This might feel like bushwhacking through a field. It can be agonizing to turn inward and change our own longstanding beliefs about how the world works, and it's never comfortable to discover personal bias or realize you might be wrong. But challenging the prejudice we hold against others, especially those who already feel marginalized or misunderstood, is how we strengthen the stakes of Zion and develop a stronger faith community.

As further light and knowledge has been revealed regarding race, gender, ethnicity, and orientation, there have been exciting changes in policy and doctrine that have helped Saints become more aligned with the true gospel of Jesus Christ. I believe each of us has a duty to stay on top of the latest teachings and guidelines. We need to operate in line with the ongoing restoration and ensure that how we serve and minister to others reflects revelation from modern-day prophets. We can't hold to old practices that keep Zion's borders closed.

---

3   *Teachings of Russell M. Nelson* (Salt Lake City: Deseret Book, 2018), 83.

4   Russell M. Nelson, "Let God Prevail," *Ensign*, November 2020.

Church leaders have been very clear that we are to "lead out in abandoning attitudes and actions of racism and prejudice"[5] and "listen to and understand what our LGBT brothers and sisters are feeling and experiencing."[6] President Russell M. Nelson was poignant and direct when he said, "I plead with you to promote respect for all of God's children."[7] In a very literal sense, following the prophet means shedding bias and promoting diversity.

In order to do this, we must first aim to suspend judgment. It's tempting to categorize other children of God, labeling them as dangerous or sinful. But Romans 3:23 reminds us that "all have sinned, and come short of the glory of God. The Savior Himself taught, "Judge not, that ye be not judged. For with what judgment ye judge, ye shall be judged: and with what measure ye mete, it shall be measured to you again" (Matthew 7:1–2).

Admittedly, I used to think people could only be lost to sin. I figured anyone who was "spiritually lost" must have made bad decisions, and needed to be called to repentance. As I've gotten older, however, I've seen that many people are actually lost to pain. I see this scenario play out often among LGBTQ Saints. Many feel judged and outcast, so they remove themselves as far as possible from people who trigger those feelings. From there, it's easy to become bitter toward the Church and never come back. Oftentimes gay individuals are viewed as sinners who "jumped off the deep end," when in reality, they are just hurt souls who never got the love and support they needed. I hate to think someone with desires to serve God might not come to church because they are scared of being judged, but

---

5   Russell M. Nelson, "Let God Prevail."

6   M. Russell Ballard, "Questions and Answers," Brigham Young University devotional, November 14, 2017.

7   Russell M. Nelson, "Let God Prevail."

it happens all the time. Gathering Israel might look less like admonishing people to change and more like getting to know them on a deep level.

> **Oftentimes gay individuals are viewed as sinners who "jumped off the deep end," when in reality, they are just hurt souls who never got the love and support they needed.**

My friend Lilly is an example of someone who was lost to pain. She spent years trying to change her orientation. She regularly fasted and prayed for God to take away her attraction to women. She forced herself to wear more makeup, walk in heels, and do anything she could to make herself more feminine. At nineteen she enrolled in sessions with a conversion therapist, who used unproven psychological methods to try to "cure" her of same-sex attraction. When she turned twenty-one, she served a full-time mission, hoping God would reward her and make her straight when she returned home. Following her missionary service, she tried desperately to date and marry a man, but she could never bring herself to commit to someone she didn't feel attracted to. Without hope for a temple marriage, she couldn't see any real place for her at church. At twenty-five years old, Lilly's worst nightmare had come true—she was lesbian, and there was nothing she could do to change it.

Lilly's mental health plummeted. She began cutting herself as punishment each time she felt attracted to a woman. She stopped praying, thinking that God must be disgusted with someone like her. In one desperate moment she told her older sister what she was going through, hoping to find a glimmer of hope from someone she loved. Instead, Lilly's sister requested that she stay away from her children, explaining that she didn't want her kids to be around someone who was "sexually confused." Lilly's depression increased, and she stopped showing up to family functions. Single, hurt, suicidal, and alone, Lilly began looking for ways to cope with her anguish. She turned to drugs, alcohol, and strangers to numb her pain. Her substance dependence made her increasingly unable to manage daily tasks, resulting in her losing her job, her apartment, and most of her friends. She was left with nothing but self-loathing, resentment, and shame.

On the surface, it would be easy for someone to look at Lilly's life and make any number of judgments. They could blame her for her bad decisions and assume she chose a sinful lifestyle. But like my Charolais cow, Lilly wasn't lost because she was wicked; she was lost because there was a hole in the fence. Her family and her ward had not afforded her the love and attention she desperately needed.

Lilly's story is not an outlier. The "pendulum swing" observed when gay people leave the Church is often a trauma response. When isolation and shame are met by a lack of support, the consequences can be dramatic and dire. We have to protect our LGBTQ friends and neighbors by loving them better. We can't afford to have such gaping holes in the fence.

My friend Becky Mackintosh, popular author and mother of a gay son, once said, "The attack on the family isn't same-sex marriage, but family contention and excluding family members over it. The adversary delights in family division, alienating children, and pushing family members outside the family circle." I share her view. The families I have seen break apart are the ones who don't accept and support their gay children. I believe the adversary was delighted with the way Lilly's family responded to her coming out. It fractured their family and left her broken and alone.

> **The families I have seen break apart are the ones who don't accept and support their gay children.**

When I found my blue-eyed cow, I knew she would want to come back to the pasture. It was a safe place where her needs were met. In the same way, we need to make our congregations places of refuge and support for lost sheep. If Lilly showed up to your ward next Sunday, how would she be accepted? Would she encounter the same rejection that pushed her away? The environment in our pasture must exceed the pull of any surrounding land.

By increasing safety and representation at Church, our pastures improve. Then, the gathering of Israel begins to fulfill itself. More welcoming spaces draw diverse people. Increased diversity weeds out cultural undercurrents that marginalize minority members. This creates a stronger sense of belonging and an overall flywheel effect.

For example, I noticed a dramatic decrease in offensive things said about gay people at church after I came out as gay. Because I was there in the room, people seemed to think twice before sharing a thought or opinion that invalidated LGBTQ people. Ward members began to challenge their beliefs, often pausing to consider if their opinions were based on fact or if they were just cultural leftovers from the past. I also saw an increase in people's desire to learn more about my identity. Rather than make blanket assumptions, many asked me about my experience with open hearts and true desires to learn. If something problematic was shared at church, these new ally members raised their hands to stand up for me and remind everyone that there is no "us vs. them" when it comes to religion and LGBTQ. This, in turn, made church feel safer for any closeted individuals in attendance, and helped all of us move closer to the true gospel of Christ.

We are gatherers, not sifters. As Elder Jeffrey R. Holland taught, "There is room for those who speak different languages, celebrate diverse cultures, and live in a host of locations. There is room for the single, for the married, for large families, and for the childless. There is room for those who once had questions regarding their faith and room for those who still do. There is room for those with differing sexual attractions."

There is room in the pasture for everyone.

Zion is not limited, unless we make it so. As Christ's covenant people, we are tasked with the gathering of Israel. President Russell M. Nelson proclaimed, "We live in a glorious age, foreseen by prophets for centuries. This is the dispensation when no spiritual blessing will be withheld from the righteous. Despite the world's commotion, the Lord would have us look forward to the future 'with joyful anticipation.' [*Teachings of Presidents of the Church: Joseph Smith* (2007), 513.] Let us not spin our wheels in the memories of yesterday. The gathering of Israel moves forward. The Lord Jesus Christ directs the affairs of His Church, and it *will* achieve its divine objectives."[8]

I want to be part of that gathering. I don't want to sit idly by.

---

8   Russell M. Nelson, "A New Normal," *Ensign*, November 2020.

If we spin our wheels in the memories of yesterday, doing the same things we have always done, we will end up with the same results. But, if we engage in the essential work of overcoming bias and finding lost hearts, Christ will use us to fulfill His divine objectives. Each soul is indispensable, and they are worth every trip through the wilderness. Let us seek to know others, mend holes in the fence, and make our pastures nurturing.

Without LGBTQ individuals, our fold is incomplete.

3.

INVITE THEM TO DINNER

I N MAY 2017, I was roaming the streets of Washington, D.C., looking for a place to live. I dedicated every waking hour to finding temporary housing for my summer internship, but every lead I found immediately fell through. I spent a few nights in the cheapest hotel I could book, and after that survived by couch surfing with a gracious stranger from the nearest young single adult ward.

Two days before my internship began, I toured a sublet I had found online. I had a really good feeling about it from the listing. It was right off DuPont Circle, my favorite neighborhood, and was surrounded by beautiful historical homes. I walked along the sidewalk under shady trees and followed the blue arrow on my phone to a colonial brick townhouse on the corner of a quiet intersection. I had let the excitement get to me, and I arrived ten minutes earlier than the listed open house. After walking a few blocks around the neighborhood to kill the time, I ran up to the buzzer and punched in the unit number.

I waited there for what seemed like hours on end, buzzing, pacing, and calling the phone number on the listing, but no one came to the door. Eventually a woman carrying groceries walked up the stoop, and I asked if she knew anything about the listing. She looked at me with a half-suspicious, half-pitiful expression and told me the unit number I had inquired about didn't exist. She said it must have been a false listing, because she owned the entire building and there were no apartments available to sublet.

I walked away crushed and overwhelmed. I had been so sure that this apartment would be the one. The big city internship I had imagined never included a vision of myself wandering streets alone or sleeping on a stranger's couch. In that moment, I felt stupid for thinking I could just up and move to a city where I had no contacts. I had looked at every listing within a thirty-minute radius at least twenty times, and was still as homeless as I was when I'd arrived. I felt like I had exhausted every option, and I had no clue what to do. After sitting there for a while, I decided to try the only approach I had left: I folded my arms and said a prayer. I told God I didn't need anything fancy, just a place where a college student could live for a summer internship. The prayer felt rather uneventful, and when I finished I resumed my daily practice of roaming the streets in search of "For Rent" signs.

Less than five minutes later I walked by a cathedral-like building with a shallow circular drive. It dominated the street, with big oak doors, four-story bay windows, and framed panels of stained glass. Near the entrance was a thick, engraved stone that sang the words "International Student House." I had one of those "look up at the sky and ask if this is real" moments, and my question was immediately confirmed by a flyer taped to the door: "Now taking summer housing applications." Within thirty minutes I had met with the housing director, filled out all necessary paperwork, and been approved to move in the following day. After going through a list of house rules, the housing director pulled out a tarnished key tied to a piece of yellow yarn.

"Before I give you this, there is one more requirement we ask of our tenants."

"What's that?" I replied, curious as to what the mysterious rule would be.

"Every night at 6:30 p.m., all students will meet in the dining hall for dinner."

"That's it?" I asked, slightly confused by her serious tone.

"That's it." She handed me the key.

I had prayed for something good, but God led me to something better.

> **I had prayed for something good, but God led me to something better.**

When I moved in the next day, I observed that the International Student House was more like a castle than a dorm. The century-old Tudor mansion that housed the students had been donated by a wealthy family, along with all original art and furniture. Arched doorways led to halls filled with early eighteenth-century paintings. A wide staircase climbed through the heart of the building, boasting rich wood molding. It opened to a welcoming but not-so-quaint library that smelled of ink and old paper. The crown jewel of the building was a spacious great hall, complete with a grand piano and views of a garden courtyard below.

I finished moving into my room that same day as the sun moved into the far quadrant of the sky. At 6:25 I put on an outfit that said "I'm trying, but I'm not trying too hard" and made my way to the dining hall for my first group dinner. I could hear the dull roar of conversation as I walked down the staircase. I felt nervous as I approached the doors—there were fifty-two tenants, and I didn't know a single one of them. I hoped I would be able to find a group I fit with.

When I walked into the bustling dining room I was met by the single most diverse group of people I have ever seen in one place. Everyone looked completely different, from a small-framed girl wearing dark clothes and a hijab to a Scandinavian giant with a full beard. It was as if each region in the world sent a twenty-three-year-old representative to sit in at dinner.

The food was served cafeteria style. I stood next to the girl in the hijab while waiting in line. She smiled at me with piercing dark eyes and said hello in a thick accent. She introduced herself and told me she was from Lahore, Pakistan. I felt almost silly telling her I was from Nowhere, Missouri. Once my plate was full I followed her to a circular table by a bay window and we sat down with her friends. As we ate, everyone went around the table to say where they were from and what brought them to D.C. Most were working at the Smithsonian museum or in the government office buildings downtown. The rest were graduate students at Georgetown, Johns Hopkins, and GWU.

As dinner wound down and people began exiting the cafeteria, a young woman came in to get food. She wore blue running shorts and looked like she was in a rush. Her box braids were tied in a tight knot and she had beads of sweat at the base of her forehead.

"That's Jasmine," said one of my new friends as he got up and left the table. "She's always running late!"

Jasmine ran to grab her food just before the cafeteria doors closed, then brought her tray over to my now empty table.

"Can I sit with you?" she asked.

"Sure!"

"Thanks, I'm starving!" she said as she scooted out a chair and introduced herself.

We spent the next two hours in the dining hall talking nonstop. Long after everyone else had left and the place had been cleaned, we stayed there laughing and telling stories. Jasmine was studying international policy at Georgetown and had been living at the student house longer than anyone else. She knew everything about everyone and gave me the rundown on who to hang out with and which nontouristy parts of the city were worth checking out.

After a while Jasmine sighed and explained that, due to a scheduling error, she had to move all of her belongings to a different room on the top floor. I didn't have anything else to do, so I offered to help. As we made our way to her room, I mentioned how diverse the dinner attendees were, and she told me the house director rarely admitted two people who were alike. Each person was there because they had some identity, characteristic, or belief that was different from everyone else. While we packed up all her belongings and carried them up multiple flights of stairs, our conversation got progressively deeper. Jasmine asked me about some of the defining moments in my life and I told her about my family's bankruptcy, my parents' divorce, and my missionary service. When I asked her the same question, I wasn't prepared for her response.

Jasmine was born in Rwanda in a time of tremendous instability. At three years old she became a refugee when war broke out between tribal groups in her home country, resulting in mass genocide. After watching her father be horrifically executed by military forces, she escaped on foot with her mother and young siblings. By miracle they survived and eventually found food and shelter at a refugee camp. Jasmine spent the next seven years moving from camp to camp, sleeping in tents and taking care of her younger siblings. She didn't find freedom until years later when she was able to immigrate to Chicago as part of a refugee placement program.

Jasmine's story made me cry multiple times. I didn't have words to express the deep sense of sorrow I felt as she shared what she had been through. Her resilience was astounding. I had only known her for a few hours, but she immediately became one of the most impressive people I had ever met. I was surprised when, later that evening, she answered a phone call and carried on a conversation in perfect Spanish. When I asked how she knew how to speak Spanish so well, she told me she had spent a few years in Andalusia just because she wanted to learn. She also spoke French, Swahili, and a Rwandan dialect called Kinyarwanda. Meeting Jasmine that night changed my heart forever and opened my mind to what I considered possible.

I was also changed by others I met while living at the International Student House. In fact, the 6:30 dinner rule taught me more than any classroom I'd ever attended. Each night I shared food with remarkable individuals from all walks of life. What Jasmine said about each resident being diverse became increasingly clear each time I ate. Everyone had a different race, gender, ethnic background, sexual orientation, religion, occupation, language, alma mater, national identity, body type, family

dynamic, or political affiliation. Some conversations were unifying and inspiring while others were heated and contentious.
It wasn't uncommon for these conversations to last far beyond
dinner and into late hours.

The beauty was that each night, no matter how impassioned
a discussion was from the day before, we all had to return to
the dining hall to share food. Once, an intern working for the
Human Rights Campaign got into a loud discussion with an
intern at the White House who was supporting anti-LGBTQ
legislation at work. They had an intense debate over policy and
human rights in conjunction with sexual orientation and gender
identity. Everyone jumped in on the conversation, from left-wing
activists to religious conservatives to Muslim art majors. Nobody
really "won" the debate that night, and the two interns each left
the dining hall enraged. I thought things would be awkward
for the rest of the summer, but the next evening I watched in
disbelief as the two of them shared a plate of butter and laughed
while they ate their bread. This became a theme throughout
the entire summer. Even after the most heated debates over
politics, racial injustice, feminism, gun laws, and religion, we
all came together as friends to share food. Dinnertime brought
us together and forced us to see the humanity in one another.

Once word got out that I was "Mormon," the news spread
fast. I was often approached by devoted members of other religions who asked questions and shared their own beliefs. I, in
turn, shared my testimony of the restoration of the priesthood
and the unique blessings available through temple covenants. On
one of my most memorable nights I found myself in a religious
conversation with a practicing Hindu from New Delhi and a
young Jewish woman from Tel Aviv. The conversation started
off rather messy. Each of us was expecting to feel attacked by

the others as we voiced our respective beliefs. We soon found, however, that we actually shared a lot of common ground, and many of the basic values and principles we held were the same. Although all three of us worshipped in different ways, we had each been formed and bettered by exercising faith and spirituality.

* * *

There's an old phrase in Christianity that says, "Love the sinner, hate the sin." Since living at the International Student House, I haven't cared for it much. Almost every one of the students I lived with had something about them I could have classified as sinful. Very few of them shared my moral code. Many of them regularly smoked or drank alcohol. Some of them were atheist, and dozens had never prayed in the name of Jesus Christ. In a normal dorm house, it would have been so easy to classify them as sinners and limit my association only to those who shared my standards.

But I didn't. Because of that simple house rule—to eat in the dining hall at 6:30 every day—my heart was expanded to a diverse cross-section of God's children who taught me how to communicate more effectively and love more deeply. Despite all the ways we were different—all the ways society put us at odds with one another—we grew in friendship and love. By associating with people who are different from me, I learned that many of the people I would have written off as "sinners" were actually beautiful children of Heavenly Parents whose backgrounds and beliefs just differed from my own. They had so much to give, and I had so much to learn. They had divine worth regardless of what they did or how they were born.

It feels problematic to me to label other people as "sinners" and go around trying to hate what they do. While I understand the good intentions behind the idea of loving the sinner and hating the sin, I feel like in practice, it perpetuates a culture of judgment and superiority. In fact, a lot of people have used those words to justify saying some pretty awful things to me and many of the people I love.

What if, instead of saying, "Love the sinner, hate the sin," we said "Love the sinner, invite them to dinner"? Sometimes we forget that we are all sinners, and we all need love and connection. One of the single greatest unifying truths of the restored gospel is that we are also all children of God. In a very real sense, we are each spiritual siblings with divine heritage. Genesis 1:27 teaches that we are made in the image of God. Imagine the impact of this simple yet profound truth! With all our different colors and kinds, each of us represents Deity. Like a photomosaic where individual pictures come together to create one overarching image, when we come together, we collectively represent God's image. Each of us has been given spiritual gifts by the great architect of our souls. The more we gather together and share these gifts, the more we can see who God is and understand His true form. We get to see different angles and sides of God as we interact with diverse cultural backgrounds and different identity traits.

> **With all our different colors and kinds, each of us represents Deity.**

As we learn from, listen to, and associate with people who are different from us, we discover more about our heavenly heritage. If we, for whatever reason, exclude demographics of God's children from associating with us, we risk missing out on much-needed growth and ultimately fail in our efforts to strengthen the stakes of

Zion. In order to create an atmosphere where God's full character can be known, we must intentionally foster an environment of love and acceptance so diversity can thrive.

In Jewish culture during the time of Christ's ministry, table rules dominated society. Who you ate with was of utmost importance. Sharing a meal with someone made a strong social statement about who you were and how devoted you were to God. Dinner signified a bond—a social acceptance—and eating with the right people was a symbol of status and righteousness. In the same way, eating with someone who was deemed unworthy was considered a defilement. Ancient Jews were incredibly selective about who was at their table, and sought to eat with only the finest, most refined guests.

The Savior was of course very aware of these social and cultural customs, but He intentionally chose to eat and commune with people who had been rejected by society. He went against the norms and shared His table with those with whom no one else was willing to eat. It wasn't just the sick or the needy, either. Christ ate with people who intentionally did not observe religious laws. He surrounded Himself with people who did not tithe, sacrifice, or observe the purity rites of the church. He shared food with people who were not allowed in the temple and befriended those who were unable or unwilling to make covenants. In order to lift others, Christ first met them where they were at.

Because of this, Jesus was viewed as scandalous. Religious people were provoked to see Christ eating with those of a lower religious class, and the Pharisees and scribes openly mocked and murmured against Him for eating with sinners (see Luke 15:1–2). He faced considerable social backlash for eating with people who were not viewed as clean, righteous, or becoming.

But Jesus didn't care. He extended these people grace, love, and acceptance, even before they repented or made covenants. He was willing to risk social standing in order to share food with people who were different from Him. His radical love and acceptance set a new precedent for what it means to love thy neighbor and is one of the defining characteristics of the Savior's ministry.

> **Christ extended people grace, love, and acceptance, even before they repented or made covenants.**

When I ponder whether I'm becoming more like the Savior, I try to think about the kinds of people I am associating with. In other words, who is at my table? Is it the gay couple who fly the Pride flag a few doors down? Is it the old acquaintance from high school who posts radically different political views on social media? Is it the single mom with face piercings and tattoos? Is it the transgender woman who hides on the back row? Is it the undocumented immigrant or the foreign refugee? In a similar way, the question can be adapted for each local ward. Who is missing from the table? Are there people of color in the congregation? Are there gay couples in the pews? For any friends and neighbors who no longer attend, do we really know their stories? Are we sure they feel completely welcome?

In order to become more like the Savior and be a true disciple of Christ, we must be willing to earnestly associate with all of God's children. We have to overcome our cultural, personal, and religious barriers and connect with those who are different from us. By doing so, we develop the character of Christ. We learn how to communicate effectively, demonstrate humility, and see each complex human as a beautiful child of God.

Luckily, we don't have to live at a house for international students to bring people to our table. Some of the great blessings we have in the modern age are the technological advances that allow us to connect. Where proximity is limited, we have resources we can use to learn more about diverse people. Books, films, and podcasts can help us learn about different identities and expand our hearts to the experiences of others. The internet and social media can connect us with varied voices all across the globe, allowing us to gain more proximity to all of God's children.

Sometimes, the voices missing from the table are the ones who make us uncomfortable. People with different religions, political ideals, or identity characteristics can seem scary or difficult to connect with, but I've found that in my life, those uncomfortable voices are often the ones I need most. Associating with people different from myself has helped me grow in my ability to love, serve, and offer empathy. Renowned anthropologist Lila Abu-Loghod once said, "Intimate familiarity with individuals anywhere makes it hard to be satisfied with sweeping generalizations about cultures, religions, or regions, or to accept the idea that problems have simple causes or solutions." I echo her sentiment. It's hard to dislike someone once you really get to know them.

On the night before my last day in the International Student House I stayed up late talking to a young woman from Southeastern India named Saanvi. She was studying to be an art curator and always wore bright, colorful clothes. After getting kicked out of the cafeteria when it was shut down for the night, she invited me up to her room to try one of her favorite treats from home—candied rose petals. We talked for hours, going over our life stories and everything we dreamed of doing.

At that point, I hadn't come out to anyone at the student house. I was worried people would view me differently, and I didn't want to heighten any cultural barriers that might already exist. But, as I was talking with Saanvi, I disclosed my orientation. I expressed how hard it was to be attracted to men when I really loved my religion. I told her how I was terrified of telling my dad and worried I would lose friends if anyone knew. She showed interest in my story and asked thoughtful follow-up questions. She said she had a friend from home that she suspected was gay, and she was worried about him as well. She said she liked being with me because I reminded her of him.

The next morning I woke up to a text from Saanvi. It said, "I know you are packing today, but if you have time, please meet me in the courtyard at 11 a.m." When I arrived, she had all of her art supplies laid out across the patio furniture. She told me I had a beautiful story, and powerful emotions, and said that feelings like that deserve to be painted. For the next two hours Saanvi taught me how to paint, guiding me as I depicted what I felt. The end result was heartbreaking, beautiful, and hauntingly true to my experience. Saanvi helped me capture feelings I'd never been able to describe, and I felt catharsis as I finished my painting. I had no idea how much I needed her to help me heal.

We live in a world that needs healing. Opinions and discussions shared online are often completely void of empathy, and face-to-face interaction is limited. News stations and media outlets filter information to drive ratings by fostering division. Information is constantly formulated to pit one person against another, and both fact and feelings are often lost in convoluted messages that drive personal agendas. In these latter days, the adversary is actively deploying elaborate, cunning schemes to divide God's children and keep us from establishing Zion. Satan breeds division and does anything he can to drive us apart.

The remedy for this plague of division is found in the teachings of Jesus Christ. The antidote to discomfort, conflict, and misunderstanding is meaningful connection. When we get to know someone's story, it shifts us. When we step away from judgment and seek to know another's heart, we develop empathy and grace. When we follow prophetic counsel to promote diversity and overcome preconceived judgments, we grow in our ability to love as the Savior loves. This promotes unity and expands the borders of Zion.

> ## The antidote to discomfort, conflict, and misunderstanding is meaningful connection.

Living at the International Student House taught me that when I view others as sinners, it impairs my ability to love them. I get blinded by the beam in my own eye and don't see their divine worth as children of God. But, when I invite them to my table, it helps me see their humanity. I learn more about God's character and marvel in the diversity He has created, thus coming to know Him more fully. Sometimes, the ones I "invite to dinner" end up feeding me, as it was with Jasmine, Saanvi, and many others.

These days, I no longer say, "Love the sinner, hate the sin." In fact, I don't even say, "Love the sinner, invite them to dinner." I just say, "Love people, invite them to dinner," and that's where I find God.

4.

SEEING DEEPLY

I N A POWERFUL Brigham Young University forum address, renowned columnist David Brooks spoke on the importance of seeing each other deeply. He said:

We have entered an age of bad generalization. We don't see each other well. We do not see the heart and soul of each person, only a bunch of bad labels. To me, this is the core problem that our democratic character is faced with. Many of our society's great problems flow from people not feeling seen and known: Blacks feeling that their daily experience is not understood by whites. Rural people not feeling seen by coastal elites. Depressed young people not feeling understood by anyone. People across the political divides getting angry with one another and feeling incomprehension. Employees feeling invisible at work. [Couples] living in broken marriages, realizing that the person who should know them best actually has no clue.

I came across this quote when Michelle D. Craig shared it as part of her October 2020 general conference address. She taught that in order to heal the polarization, hatred, and pain among us, we must begin to see each other deeply. She connected this concept to the way the Savior ministered. She taught, "Jesus Christ sees people deeply. . . . Where others saw fishermen, sinners, or publicans, Jesus saw disciples; where others saw a man possessed by devils, Jesus looked past the outward distress, acknowledged the man, and healed him."[9] This became a pattern throughout the Savior's ministry. When blessing and healing individuals, Christ first began by acknowledging the divinity in the afflicted person and accepting them as they were. Seeing them deeply was the gateway that allowed them to be healed.

> **In order to heal the polarization, hatred, and pain among us, we must begin to see each other deeply.**

During my undergrad at BYU, I was on the trampoline dunk team. We performed halftime entertainment at sporting events, wowing the crowds with synchronized basketball routines using mini trampolines. With perfectly timed lines, we flipped and twisted through the air, passing basketballs in tandem, then culminating in jaw-dropping dunks. After performances at late weekend games, my teammates and I religiously went to a twenty-four-hour breakfast diner on the far side of town. It was dingy and the food was terrible, but it was cheap, open late, and we were usually the only patrons. It was the perfect place to loosen

---

9   Michelle D. Craig, "Eyes to See," *Ensign*, November 2020.

up and unwind after a long week, and we could be as loud and rowdy as we wanted.

One night, packed around a sticky table underneath stark fluorescent lighting, a waitress came by to deliver our food. She looked tired and disheveled. She was odd, seemed a little spacey, and almost dropped one of our plates. It took her what seemed like an eternity to get our food passed to the table, and as she sauntered off we snickered because every single order was wrong. We were also missing silverware and straws. We never went to the diner expecting a gourmet experience, but something about this particular waitress seemed especially strange.

She came back into the dining area to check on our table a few minutes later and we finally got our silverware. She wore an orange dress and a stained white apron. Her name tag said Ricky but she told us her name was Franky. I refrained from making a joke about how the names were so similar that it didn't really matter anyway. She seemed timid, but she asked about our matching navy polos and we told her about our team and our latest performance. My buddies joked about how I was the only one to miss a dunk. She stifled a laugh. We ate, she brought our check, and we all left.

The next day was stake conference. As I listened, my stake president issued a challenge. He invited us to think about someone in our lives we would never envision being friends with. He promised that if we took the time to get to know them, we would be blessed. As he spoke, I thought of a strange, orange-aproned girl with a boy's name. I decided to take his challenge and befriend Franky.

The following evening I went to a convenience store across the street from my apartment to buy cereal and milk for a late-night study snack. When I walked in I was greeted by a short cashier dressed in all black with a beanie pulled tightly over her head. I noticed a few strands of hair that stuck out around her ears, dyed neon green. I went to the back of the small store to get my groceries. At the checkout I saw that the girl had been drawing in a sketchbook. She was working on some sort of half woman, half wolf, anime creature. She messed up when she scanned the milk and had to void the receipt. She reminded me of Franky.

The next night I went back to the convenience store to buy more snacks. I grabbed a pack of neon gummy worms and offered them to her with a joke about "neon worms to match her neon hair." Her cheeks flushed bright pink, but she accepted my gift with a nervous laugh and a thank you. She told me her name was Becca.

On Friday nights at the diner, I made sure Franky was our server every time. I tried my best to compliment her service, which surprisingly kept getting better. I asked her about her day, included her in our funny stories, and listened while she talked about her dog. Sometimes she brought out an extra milkshake or two for the table. Before long we found ourselves talking about her during the week at practice and looking forward to seeing her after every game. The whole team started keeping up with Franky.

In the meantime, I kept going back to the convenience store to talk to Becca. I bought her the same gummy worms every time I went. She usually seemed unsure of herself and shy, but one night she let me flip through her sketchbook. She drew animals and people with eyes you could swim in. Her characters had personalities that could be felt through her contrasting pencil strokes. I'd never really liked anime style, but I loved flipping through her pages. She had a deep understanding of shape, shading, and form. She was brilliantly talented. I started taking one of my friends to the store with me so he could get to know Becca too.

The more Friday nights we spent together, the more I realized that Franky was an absolute riot. Even though my teammates and I were the only late-night regulars, she made a big poster that said "Reserved for BYU Boys" and put it in our favorite spot every time there was a weekend ball game. She started joining in on our jokes and revelry, shooting straw wrappers across the room and timing us as we chugged orange juice. One time I invited her to take home half of an uneaten pie, but she wouldn't have it. She said she took home so much pie that sometimes she just put it in the oven to make her kitchen smell good, then threw it away. I snorted out my drink and asked if she'd ever heard of a candle. That night she came to check on our table about every three minutes. We teased her by telling her to just pull up a chair.

One night at the convenience store I asked Becca if she would show me her hair. She had worn the same beanie every time I saw her. She braced herself with a tight-lipped sigh, then slid the beanie off of her head to reveal a wild, jagged pixie cut with sweeping bangs. I had expected her hair to be all green, and was surprised to see it fall out in a vivid rainbow pattern. She was a neon rainbow flag.

Becca opened up to me. She told me that she cut her hair and dyed it when she came out to herself as bisexual, but she only took the beanie off when she was alone or with very close friends. I was one of the first people outside of that circle to see her hair. She told me she felt misunderstood by her family and trapped by the culture in Utah. She was scared of getting fired from her job. She didn't know what her future would look like, and she often felt unsafe.

I came out to Becca, too. At that point, I hadn't trusted the information with hardly anyone. In many ways, I felt exactly like her. We talked about what it was like to be part of the LGBTQ community in Utah. We talked about hiding parts of our personalities in public and how scary it felt. We talked about how frustrating it was to feel judged or discriminated against for something we had absolutely no control over. We talked about what it was like to not get the same rights, privileges, or treatment as other people simply because we were born outside of the norm.

I saw myself in her, and she saw herself in me.

The next day I got a text from Becca asking me to stop by the store. I walked in later that evening and she showed me a picture she'd been working on all day. It was me as a rainbow puppy dog. It was the weirdest, kindest, most beautiful thing I had ever seen.

Some nights later we went to the diner, eager to take our usual table and joke around with Franky, but our poster wasn't there. We sat down and waited for her to come out to take our order, but instead we were approached by an older woman who worked back in the kitchen. She told us Franky had quit her job earlier in the week and most likely wouldn't be returning. Everyone was visibly affected by the news, and I felt a deep sense of loss. Hanging out with Franky had become one of my favorite parts of the week.

The woman slipped an envelope out of her apron and asked, "Which one of you is Charlie?" I raised my hand and she passed it to me. On the outside, in scratchy handwriting it said, "BYU Boys."

I opened the envelope to find a hand-written thank you card. I read it out loud to the table.

Franky told us about her life. She said she grew up in a difficult family with a lot of hardships. She never felt like she fit in, and she dropped out of school because people had told her she was too stupid to ever do anything worthwhile. She ended up taking the job at the diner as a last resort, and thought she would be stuck there forever. She wrote that we, the "BYU Boys," were the first people to ever really show interest in her. We were the first people to give her compliments and make her feel like she had worth. She thanked us for making her feel like part of our group and for helping her see the value she has to offer.

In the letter, Franky said our friendship had inspired her to go back to school. She had been saving up money and found a new job in a different city that would work better with her schedule and allow her to take night classes. She said she would really miss us, but she was off to bigger and better things. I noticed how her handwriting got looser and sloppier as it went, as if she were writing faster and faster. It was visible evidence at how excited she was to go back to school and take on new challenges. I couldn't contain my smile.

Enclosed in the card was a twenty-dollar bill with a note that said, "The pie's on me tonight, boys. Charlie, if you can't finish it, take it home and put it in the oven," followed by a winky face. We sat in silence for a bit, processing Franky's letter. Then, we all broke out into hoops, hollers, and competing conversations:

"Franky is so cool!"

"I'm so proud of her!"

"I'm going to miss her!"

"She's better than all of us combined!"

After dinner (and a big, beautiful pie for dessert), we said our goodbyes and walked out into the parking lot. I got in my car, clicked on the inside light, and pulled out Franky's letter.

I re-read it three times, and I cried.

A few weeks later when I went to see Becca, she wasn't there either. I texted to ask if her schedule had changed, and she told me she was packed up in a U-Haul and moving to Texas. She wanted a new start where she could feel more accepted by her community, and when she found a job opening in Austin, she immediately applied. It all unfolded so fast. She had already left because she didn't want to have to say goodbye. I expressed my happiness that things had worked out and sent my best wishes. She texted me a picture she had drawn of me and the friend I brought to the store and thanked me for being one of the only people in Utah she felt comfortable around.

I was almost ashamed to think the reason I took interest in Franky and Becca was because of the challenge. I felt unworthy to accept the gratitude they expressed for our friendship, since I felt I had benefitted so much more. My stake president was right, though: my life was blessed by getting to know them. My initial impression was that they were weird and we would never be friends. But as I sought to know them, that immediately changed. I was amazed how they let me in with little or no reservations. They were peculiar, for sure, but they didn't hide it. That opened my heart in unexpected ways, and we were all better for it. By seeing them deeply, they experienced healing, and so did I.

After meeting Franky and Becca, I wanted to become more like them—willing to be seen deeply. At that point in time, I had spent years hiding an integral aspect of my identity. When I was a child and felt a strange pull toward men, I didn't tell anyone. When I hit puberty and realized that "strange pull" was attraction to my same gender, I buried those feelings deep inside me and wrapped them in a sandblasted coat of shame. As I grew older, having someone see me deeply was my greatest fear. I built a fortress of impenetrable walls around that tender, terrifying part of me. I wove intricate webs of lies that were so convincing that, at some levels, I almost believed them myself.

My fear of letting others see me deeply manifested in strange and heartbreaking ways. I remember being terrified to get my wisdom teeth taken out. I wasn't scared of dry sockets, blood clots, or jaw soreness. I was scared I would tell someone I was gay while under anesthesia. I trained myself to "check girls out" as they walked past me, internally disturbed by perpetuating the objectification of women, but relieved each time a buddy would smirk and say, "Hey, hey! I saw that!" I even pretended my teenage obsession with Taylor Swift was simply because she was hot, not because I was enthralled by her poetic mind and living vicariously through her emotional songs about what it was like to date a boy.

In the most unnatural way, pretending to be something I wasn't became as natural as breathing. It was a constant under-current—a filter that colored every aspect of my life. To break the facade and let someone know who I actually was felt like an impossibility. I would rather have died than admit I was gay. Keeping my secret safe behind a barrage of walls seemed like the only way I could ever go on.

> **I would rather have died than admit I was gay.**

But the secret made me sick. It was a cancer that ate through me. By the time I was home from a mission and expected to date, marry, and start a family, holding on to my secret was crushing my ability to connect with the people I loved most. I spent so much time and energy trying to reconcile my faith with my orientation that I could hardly be myself around my family and friends. I lived in a constant lie, which compounded the depression, anxiety, and shame I had shouldered since I was a child.

I needed to tell someone—to let them in and begin the healing process—but the weight of my "what ifs" was colossal. I was burdened by impossibly difficult questions: What if my family rejected me? What if my relationships changed? What if my friends treated me differently? What if I lost trust from people I love? What if my family was embarrassed? What if I wasn't allowed to participate at church? What if I got kicked out of BYU? What if nobody respected my testimony? There was only one way to know the answer to those questions, and it came at the cost of sharing a secret I could never take back.

But I knew being seen deeply led to healing, and that need outweighed the fears that plagued me. I started by telling my cousin Rachel, one of the safest, most accepting people I know. She was kind, patient, and told me she loved me exactly as I am. She asked thoughtful questions and spent hours learning about my experience without any filters. She helped me see my worth as a child of God and exhibited hope and empathy greater than I've ever known. Rachel was the first person to break through my guarded walls and see me deeply. She was the agent that set me on a trajectory to heal.

Like Rachel, each of my family members met me with love and respect when I let them see me deeply. My sister Janine told me she would be my biggest cheerleader, and my sister Anne said she would be whatever I needed her to be. One by one, each member of my family gave me the love and support I needed. Since then they have each put extraordinary effort into learning about who I am and how I fit into the world. They have spent countless hours listening to my experiences as a gay member of the Church. They have listened to podcasts, read books, and studied scriptures in order to know how to best understand me. They have asked me about who I'm attracted to, stood up for me to their friends, and changed their schedules to hear me speak. They haven't just sought to know about my orientation; they have sought to know my heart. They know and love the realest, deepest, most raw version of me. Any shame and embarrassment I have cannot withstand the power of their love.

I'm often asked why gay people feel the need to come out. There are some very practical reasons. For starters, orientation is often necessary information to convey. In society, the general assumption is that everyone is straight. This gets pretty awkward if you're not. That's why straight people don't have to come out and gay people do. Each time someone tries to set me up on a date or asks what I'm looking for in a girlfriend, it's appropriate to mention my orientation and let them know I'm not romantically interested in women. So much of our culture is based on relationships and dating, and life is a lot easier when the people around me know I'm gay. There's also a community aspect to coming out. It's validating to meet other people who are like you and who have experienced similar triumphs and challenges. Connecting with other gay individuals has helped me feel belonging and led me to lifelong friends.

But I believe the real reason people come out is to be seen deeply. For me, the phrase "coming out to someone" can be used interchangeably with "letting someone in." It allowed how others see me to become congruent with who I really am. It freed me from the burdens of shame and self-loathing I carried, and I was able to develop deeper relationships instead of putting up walls. Though some people meet much more backlash and have much more stressful coming-out experiences, each queer person I know has experienced similar blessings and relief through coming out. LGBTQ people don't come out for attention; they come out to be freed from living a lie.

> **The phrase "coming out to someone" can be used interchangeably with "letting someone in."**

There is a fascinating scripture, 1 John 3:2, that teaches what the Saints will be like when Christ comes again. It says: "It doth not yet appear what we shall be: but we know that, when [Christ] shall appear, we shall be like him; for we shall see him as he is." I have adopted this scripture for when I think about my future as a gay member of the Church. When it comes to LGBTQ and the Church of Jesus Christ, I'm not sure what is going to happen. There is no way to know what revelation will be given or what policy changes might be enacted or reinforced. I do know, however, that the way to bridge the divide that exists between LGBTQ individuals and The Church of Jesus Christ of Latter-day Saints is to see others deeply. We must become experts at exercising humility and compassion and have brave conversations that honor both identity and testimony. We must learn to throw out preconceived notions and offer grace as we connect with each other.

As Sister Sharon Eubank said, "We may not yet be where

5.

ALL OF US

'LL NEVER FORGET THE FRENZY my middle school basketball team made over one particular seat on the bench. Our
coach could be quite the hothead. Each time a player in the
game made a careless foul or a foolish turnover, he had a habit
of pulling whoever was directly next to him to sub in. If he was
in the right mood (meaning, the wrong mood), it didn't matter
if you were a B-team player. If you were in that coveted spot, he
would grab you by the elbow and throw you toward the score
table. The worst player on the team could go right in for one
of the starting five. Naturally, after every time-out there was a
mad rush among the players. Everyone wanted to sit right next
to the coach.

Everyone except me.

I would never have admitted it, but having a clear view of the
cheerleaders was much more important to me than playing in
the game. In our home gym, I discovered that if I sat in the ninth
seat down, I would always be right across from Kaley Evans,

the best flyer on the squad. Sitting directly across from her was always the highlight of my night. It gave me an unobstructed view of her balancing on one foot atop a pyramid, or spinning her body down into a cradle to be caught.

For the next five years I saw posters for cheer tryouts go up every spring. I would stare at the posters, memorize the date and time, and hate myself for not being able to go. There were typical barriers—I wasn't very strong, I didn't have technical training, my parents didn't have enough money to pay gym fees, I was too busy with school and other sports—but deep down I knew the real reason I never tried out for cheer.

Pretending to be somebody else was so necessary that, in time, it didn't even feel like a chore. My life was a constant cycle of making sure to never do anything that anyone would perceive as gay. This meant hiding my music taste, never crossing my legs, and making sure to dress and speak as ordinarily and masculine as possible in public. I even used old brown paper grocery bags to make covers for some of the books I read. Normal, straight guys didn't read teenage vampire romance novels.

Maybe another guy from my hometown could have joined the cheer squad. If he got bullied for being "fruity," he could defend himself. Maybe for him it would even have been cool. But not me. I was actually attracted to men. I had to do everything I could to make sure I wasn't sniffed out, and that meant being on the basketball team instead of cheering for it. In the privacy of my own backyard I taught myself how to dance, trick, and tumble, but for years I kept those talents far from the public eye.

As a college undergrad, millions of people across the globe saw me flip and dance as Cosmo the Cougar. I won hearts and inspired fans by performing those same moves I used to hide in my backyard. It was incredible to see how many people embraced my character as the mascot, but even then, I was always safely behind a mask. I found ways to infuse Cosmo with my own flare, but always while playing the part of a strong, football-loving, hypermasculine mountain lion. My job was to become something other people would like. And I was good at it, because I'd been doing it since I was three years old. But as I basked in the strange glory of anonymous stardom, I still feared that if I ever removed my other mask and let people see the real me, I would lose everything. So, in my personal life, I kept living behind it, working hard to make sure no one discovered I was gay.

By the time I overcame my shame and came out publicly, I had quite the list of regrets. For fear of looking like a stereotype and outing myself, there were so many things I had never done. So, at twenty-five years old, I created a "retroactive bucket list" as a way to reclaim the childhood experiences I'd never let myself have. One by one I went through it, judging pageants, taking ballet classes, and crossing my legs whenever the heck I wanted. But there was one thing on the list I thought I'd never get to check off . . . Cheer.

While deciding my next step after living in New York for a few years, I felt a strong pull to further my education. It felt important to move back to Utah and become a mental health professional. As I was touring and applying for different programs across the state, I met up with some of my old dunk team buddies at a gymnastics gym to tumble. While there, I was introduced to a BYU cheerleader. She taught me the basics of partner stunting and, naturally, I was hooked. When I learned she was starting a master's program my jaw dropped. I had no idea graduate students were still eligible for sports.

A few months and a tryout later, I was the newest member of BYU's coed cheer squad. I no longer had to sit on the bench to get a view of the cheerleaders; they flew right above my head! The first few weeks were grueling as I learned how to throw, catch, and balance flyers in the air, but through every sprained finger and bloody nose, I was delighted to be part of the team. When the season started up, I was back on the sidelines where I belonged, but this time, without the mask. The green grass, bright lights, and roar of the crowd felt familiar, yet the experience was new. I was no longer dancing on the field in a cougar suit. Instead, I was throwing people in the air, running flags, leading yells, and shooting T-shirts to the crowd with a Gatling gun.

A lot of people viewed me as "BYU's gay cheerleader," and I welcomed it. As word got around, that reputation helped me connect with people and minister to others. At a home basketball game, I was approached by a couple whose youngest daughter was lesbian. They said she wasn't doing well and asked for advice on how to help her feel valued and loved. I offered suggestions and connected them with mental health resources for their family. During a football game in Spokane, Washington, a fan came up to me at halftime. She told me her little brother was gay and had just applied for BYU. She had been concerned about him having a negative experience but said that seeing me helped ease her worry. Once, I was even stopped by a fan from the University of Utah, our rival school. He said seeing me cheer inspired him to reach out to an old mission companion he hadn't talked to since the companion had come out and married a man. The fan and his wife made plans to get lunch with the former companion and his husband. His face lit up as he told me how excited he was to reconnect. I was amazed to see how many opportunities I found to serve, just by showing up as myself.

> **I was amazed to see how many opportunities I found to serve, just by showing up as myself.**

During my final year, our cheer team was determined to compete at nationals. It had been a decade since the team had been strong enough to contend, and our school had long since been forgotten on the nationals stage, but we were a squad of grit, resolution, and talent. Our coaches held intra-team try-outs, and I was selected along with nineteen other individuals to compete on mat.

Before long, the stress and pressure of training for nationals began to wear on us. In addition to schooling, jobs, and regular cheer practices and appearances, we had to learn and execute a highly skilled routine, complete with elite stunts, jump sequences, synchronized tumbling passes, and a complicated pyramid. We woke up long before sunrise, conditioning our bodies, putting in extra practices, and recuperating in the athletic training room. Various injuries meant other teammates had to step in, requiring the whole team to adjust to any differences. The physical, mental, and emotional toll of nationals prep was colossal.

As we trained, I found I could be an asset far beyond my stunting or tumbling abilities. Thanks in part to my orientation, I was able to develop special relationships with the female athletes. Many of them shared personal challenges with me, dropping all emotional walls. I was able to offer empathy, encouragement, and advice without them ever wondering if I would mistake our friendship for something more. At the same time, as a man, I was able to connect and communicate well with the other men on the team. I could act as a liaison between my teammates and operate free from social barriers that sometimes accompany coed sports. By just being myself, I was able to increase morale and drive team unity.

After four months of preparation, palm trees and salty air welcomed us to Daytona Beach. We were underdogs, competing in the largest coed division, but we were hungry. In order to make finals we had to place high in the preliminary competition. Adrenaline pumped through my body as we walked into the arena, sending a simultaneous rush of nerves and excitement. Cheerleaders were everywhere, with giant bows and sparkly, teased-up hair. After a blur of warm-ups, run-throughs, and team prayers, BYU was announced and we ran through a curtain onto the nationals stage.

Bright spotlights blasted the cheer floor, making everything beyond it pitch-black. If not for the screaming crowd, I might have thought the twenty of us on the mat were the only people in the world. I could feel my heart pumping as I took starting position with my flyer. The music began with a sudden beat, marking my cue to begin. I threw my partner in the air, twisting her around and catching her on one foot, high above my head. This opening stunt always caused me the most worry, but it hit perfectly. Once I placed her back on the ground, I transitioned to my standing tumbling pass with an enormous, open-mouthed smile. I felt unstoppable.

We all had different backgrounds, different skills, and different bodies, but every single person was needed in order to hit the routine. Collective success could not be achieved without each individual's uniqueness. There was one teammate who wasn't the most elite tumbler, but without her height and strength, our pyramid would fall. Another struggled with dance moves but could twist through the air like a tornado. The diversity of our personalities and talents was essential to hit a winning routine. Everyone had to nail their specific role.

The coaches and choreographers had played to my own strengths, placing me in traditionally female positions to draw eyes from the judges. While my other male teammates threw a basket toss, I joined the ladies in a triple toe-touch jump sequence. When the guys moved back to pose during the dance portion, I strutted up the middle in a series of sassy choreography. I competed as the cheerleader I had always dreamed of being, on a grand stage I never could have imagined.

Amidst sharp motions and vibrant facial expressions, I watched my teammates through peripheral vision, checking for potential deductions. But I didn't see any. Every stunt group sailed through each elite-level move with perfect synergy.

When we hit our final pose the crowd erupted.

Dazed, dizzy, and breathing heavy, we rushed backstage to meet our coaches and joined in euphoric celebration. We pressed ourselves around a table to watch an instant replay. I kept a sharp eye out for deductions or falls I may have missed, but I still couldn't identify a single one. The video ended with a slightly pixelated version of me, center panel, fist pumping in celebration and wrapping a teammate next to me in a bear hug.

Had BYU cheer hit their first ever perfect nationals routine?

Moments later a scoresheet confirmed: We had.

We received zero deductions from any judge, and we continued to finals with the highest overall score.

* * *

When I think back on my time as a BYU cheerleader, that one, perfect moment stands out above the rest. It's not because of the scoresheet, or even the thrill of a flawless routine. The nationals performance was exceptional because each individual gave their whole heart. All of us competed with everything that we are.

Our differences made us stronger. Had each teammate been the same, or tried to blend in with the others, we never could have achieved such greatness. Success came only as we were true to ourselves and confident in the contributions each unique individual could solely make.

The Apostle Paul taught this same concept in reference to the body of Christ. 1 Corinthians 12:14–18 reads, "For the body is not one member, but many. If the foot shall say, Because I am not the hand, I am not of the body; is it therefore not of the body? And if the ear shall say, Because I am not the eye, I am not of the body; is it therefore not of the body? If the whole body were an eye, where were the hearing? If the whole were hearing, where were the smelling? But now hath God set the members every one of them in the body, as it hath pleased him."

God doesn't just need all of us to build Zion; He needs all of each of us—every aspect of our divine creation.

> ## God doesn't just need all of us to build Zion; He needs all of each of us.

Honoring my full self, including my orientation, allows me to serve as part of the body of Christ. Since coming out as gay, I'm often posed with the question, "But what about your covenants?" It seems what people are usually asking is, "What about the law of chastity?" How disappointing is that question? It doesn't seem to be asked of straight members of the Church—at least not with the same connotation. But because I am attracted to men, everyone seems to boil my covenants down to only "not having sex." They overlook the many other incredibly personal, sacred promises I have made with God. In fact, when I think about my covenants, sex is one of the last things that comes to mind.

To give my time, talents, and efforts, I have to give my whole self. I can't build the kingdom of God and establish Zion if I'm an "ear" trying to be an "eye." This means, in order to fully keep my covenants, I have to accept and honor the part of me that's attracted to men. By doing so, I have learned how to better mourn with those that mourn and comfort those who stand in need of comfort. I have made important sacrifices that align with personal revelation and God's will. I've been required to exercise more grace, patience, and obedience than I ever thought possible.

One of the most meaningful covenants I have made is to take the name of Jesus Christ upon myself. In order to do this, I have to be one hundred percent me. I can't take the name of Christ upon a me who is pretending to be somebody else.

In the Sermon on the Mount, the Savior taught, "Ye are the salt of the earth: but if the salt have lost his savour, wherewith shall it be salted? it is thenceforth good for nothing, but to be cast out, and to be trodden under foot of men. Ye are the light of the world. A city that is set on an hill cannot be hid. Neither do men light a candle, and put it under a bushel, but on a candlestick; and it giveth light unto all that are in the house. Let your light so shine before men, that they may see your good works, and glorify your Father which is in heaven." (Matthew 5:13–16).

Each LGBTQ individual has unique gifts and contributions that all of us need. Heartbreakingly, many feel pressure to dim their light and lose the savor of their salt. That social pressure caused a younger me to warm the bench on a basketball team instead of shine on a cheer squad. Instead of giving my hometown what I gave to BYU, I crammed myself into societal expectations. By hiding unique aspects of my personality and keeping the status quo, my efforts were "good for nothing."

When I was hiding my orientation under a bushel, I was also hiding parts of my personality, and I couldn't fulfill the measure of my creation. There were countless times I saw opportunities to beautify and improve things around me, but for fear of being labeled or rejected, I sat on the bench. From talking to other LGBTQ members of the Church, this seems to be a common thread. They feel pressured to not be themselves, so they aren't, and the world misses out on their talents and gifts. In turn, they miss out on self-actualization, and everyone loses light and salt.

If for shame, embarrassment, or fear, we hide our gifts, we cannot be instruments in the Lord's hands. Our capacity to serve and keep covenants is diminished because our thoughts are turned inward. But, when we courageously show up as ourselves, we add to the beauty of the world and can "multiply, and replenish the earth" (Genesis 1:28). Subsequently, we can help others feel more comfortable with themselves, too. Being authentic fosters an environment where all can take their respective place on the cheer mat, and serve with "all [their] heart, might, mind and strength" (D&C 4:2).

Elder Jeffrey R. Holland taught, "The first great *truth* in the universe is that God *loves us* exactly that way—wholeheartedly, without reservation or compromise, with all of *His* heart, might, mind, and strength. And when those majestic forces from His heart and ours meet without restraint, there is a veritable explosion of spiritual, moral power. Then, as Teilhard de Chardin wrote, 'for [the] second time in the history of the world, man will have discovered fire.'"[11]

As a BYU Cheerleader, I discovered that fire. It burned every instant I supported a teammate and each time I connected with a fan. It even burned when I danced, tumbled, and did toe-touches at nationals. I was able to uplift, entertain, perform, and serve at my highest potential because I was completely myself.

I'll never know the full impact of me being an out, gay cheerleader at BYU. I do know that every weekend sixty thousand people saw me cheering on the sidelines, and somewhere, in the crowd, was at least one little boy like me, watching the cheerleaders. Maybe, because I finally found the courage to be myself, he will never have to hide who he is. His time, talents, and efforts can build God's kingdom through his own unique personality, and he won't have to wait twenty-five years to brighten and flavor the world.

We expand the borders of Zion when we serve with our full self—all of us.

---

11 Jeffrey R. Holland, "The Greatest Possession," *Liahona*, November 2021.

6.

A PLACE TO BELONG

WHEN I WAS YOUNG, my mom ordered a cassette tape of Primary singalong songs. My older sisters and I would scream-sing along at the top of our lungs every time we loaded up in the back of her maroon Buick LeSabre. Thinking back on how much we listened to it, I have no idea how she managed. If I had three kids screaming "I belong to The Church of Jesus Christ of Latter-day Saints" every time I drove my car, I can almost guarantee the cassette would suffer a tragic "accident." But my mom let us sing, and by doing so helped me internalize simple truths and learn about my religious identity.

I probably sang those words over a thousand times: "I belong to The Church of Jesus Christ of Latter-day Saints." I liked the visuals that came with the phrase. I thought of my local church meetinghouse, with its 70s orange brick and its giant white steeple set against a low, sweeping roofline. I thought of the carpeted gym where I did cartwheels and played basketball. I thought of my sisters pushing me on the giant vacuum as we cleaned the empty building on Saturday mornings, and of what might lie in the mysterious attic space above the custodial closet. I thought of the organ pipes in the chapel, and how I loved to feel the deep, bass-coupled notes of hymns vibrate through my chest during sacrament meetings on Sunday. The building was as much my home as any place in the world.

But it wasn't just the building that held my heart. I felt a sense of safety and familiarity among the people in my ward. I loved attending early morning seminary and learning about the scriptures. I enjoyed passing and preparing the sacrament to other members of my congregation. There weren't many Latter-day Saints in the area where I grew up, so church became a refuge as I got older. Being "the Mormon kid" at school meant constantly swimming against the current, but at church I was surrounded by people with similar values who honored my beliefs. Before I confronted my orientation, I belonged to the Church, and the Church belonged to me. As I grew older and began to accept who I am, however, I discovered that belonging *to* The Church of Jesus Christ was very different from belonging *in* The Church of Jesus Christ.

When I was a child, my orientation didn't seem to matter much. It had no effect on my ability to be involved at church, and nobody there knew about it. I myself barely understood what it was and the impact it would have. As I grew older, however, my orientation began to feel like a wedge planted in the tree of my faith. My testimony and my church participation grew in spite of it, twisting limbs and branches around its sharp edges and burying it deep within me. From the outside I looked like every other tree at church, and I threw myself into the luxury of letting people think I was. Ironically, in some ways, my orientation helped me blend in. I was praised for how righteous and respectful I was for being more interested in school and spirituality than in going on dates with girls. Parents and leaders never worried about my conduct, and because I was running away from myself, I was almost always anxiously engaged in a good cause. Despite the internal and spiritual challenges posed by hiding my orientation, I truly felt like I belonged.

But that sense of belonging shattered when I returned home from serving a mission. Once I was expected to seriously pursue marriage and family, that hidden wedge began to split my branches. I was flooded with questions about dating and marriage. Marital status determined everything, from who my friends were to which ward I attended. Religion professors chided that it was the only way to exaltation. Sunday School lessons centered around dating. Friends and family members asked me who I was going out with and when I would settle down with my special someone.

I went on hundreds of dates with the most incredible women in the world, but felt no romantic feelings whatsoever. The shame and isolation from my long-kept secret festered inside me. I began viewing myself as an outcast and felt like there was no way anyone could ever accept me for who I truly was. The congregations that once championed me now made me feel like an outsider. The same pews, chapels, and walls that once felt like home now felt like a cage of thorns.

Naturally, I began having real, serious issues with beliefs that had never bothered me before. As a child, the doctrine of eternal families was incredibly dear to me, as it meant I could be with my beloved family members for time and all eternity. As an adult, however, the expectation to start a new eternal family by marrying a woman and having children riddled me with anxiety. I felt like the entire gospel was set up with the singular objective of forcing me to fail. I tried to cling to the Church and suffocate my identity, but everything around me screamed, "You do not belong here."

I wrestled for several years with the burning question of whether or not I could reconcile my orientation with my spiritual and religious beliefs. That process required me to reach deep within myself and reconstruct large portions of my faith and my worldview. Although it was arduous and painful, as I examined my individual creation and my personal relationship with Deity, I began to accept myself for who I am and grow in my ability to see God within me. I became more proficient at separating Church culture from gospel doctrine, reclaimed spiritual experiences from childhood, and gained a real testimony that I have a place within God's kingdom.

Strangely, however, even when I felt like I belonged with God, I didn't feel like I belonged at Church. I felt an inverse correlation between my personal healing—my learning to finally accept and honor my orientation and trust God with it—and my social standing within the Church. God worked better after coming out, but Church had worked better in the closet. As I accepted who I am and stopped hiding my orientation, I felt more and more estranged. Congregational and institutional dynamics didn't seem to care that I was happier and healthier than ever. People viewed me as an outsider, and my Sunday worship was invariably coupled with insecurity.

> **God worked better after coming out, but Church had worked better in the closet.**

I started feeling like there was an expiration date on my church participation. Each time I took the sacrament or went to the temple, I was crossed by the intrusive thought, "I wonder if this is the last time I will be able to do this." Religion seemed fleeting, not because of any choices I was making, but due to the thwarted belonging that so comprehensively defined my experience. By the time I graduated from college in 2018 and was out on my own, longevity in the Church felt like a pipe dream—a vast cavern of pyrite pretending to be gold.

I ended up moving to New York City. I settled in well, with an exciting job at an international security firm and a place I split with my dad on the Upper East Side. One Thursday while at work, my phone lit up with a message from the ward bulletin. I opened it to see a reminder for stake temple night. I felt a slight kick in my stomach—a reminder of how conflicted I felt about church.

I ignored the message and kept working.

A little while later I took a break and looked out the window. My office building sat on the southeast corner of Central Park, and from the thirtieth floor the winding pathways and bushy treetops made it look more like a scale model than a real park. Lakes and small ponds glittered against the dark green of the shrubbery, and pedestrians walked around like ants down below. From my vantage point I could see across to the west side of the city. I scanned the skyline until my gaze lingered on a skyscraper right across from the temple. Truthfully it wasn't that far of a walk. I knew if I worked fast I could still make it to stake temple night.

But I wasn't sure if I wanted to go.

Though my Manhattan YSA ward was one of the most accepting congregations I'd ever encountered, I still didn't feel like I belonged in the Church at large. There were so many things I didn't understand and so many ways I felt excluded. I was sick of trying so hard to belong in the Church only to be repeatedly disappointed by continual reminders of all the ways in which I didn't, couldn't, and would never fit in. I was tired of feeling like there was nobody else like me and feeling like my future in the Church hinged on whether or not I was married to a woman in the temple—something that was never going to happen.

So what was the point in going?

I played out the scenario in my mind: I would go to the temple, feel awkward the whole time, get frustrated, feel guilty for my frustration, then walk home alone.

Stellar.

Not worth it.

But the "Stake Temple Night" group chat kept buzzing through the afternoon. Each message sent a shot of anxiety through me. I found myself pacing back and forth by my desk, wondering if I should go. I reflected on how easy the temple used to be for me. I remembered my first time doing baptisms for the dead as a twelve-year-old. I had made the three-and-a-half-hour trip to St. Louis with a group of youth from my home ward. Walking into the temple felt mystical and surreal. Every part of the experience was full of anticipation, but there was a calmness that resonated within me. I spent time praying, reading scripture, and reflecting as I waited in the small chapel room outside the baptismal font. Later, as I watched others through the large glass window while I waited to be baptized, I had the overwhelming sense I was exactly where I needed to be. It was a powerful moment that grounded me in my faith.

Those days felt like a lifetime ago.

As I wrapped up the workday, I muted the ward group chat and signed up for a workout class at my gym. I figured it would be a good way to keep my mind off things. As I went down the elevator and walked out the revolving doors onto 5th Avenue, however, the decision felt like a rock in my shoe. I felt weird going to a workout class when my heart wanted to be in the temple. Eventually I assessed the situation and decided that if I didn't feel comfortable going inside the temple, I could at least go look at the building in a sort of "Sorry God, I wish I could do this but I don't fit in here" kind of half-worship. I started walking west across the park toward Lincoln Square.

Once there, I sat down on the edge of a large fountain. I looked over my surroundings. Entrance lines for the orchestra snaked across the plaza, comprised of hundreds of people with their heads buried in cell phones. I heard blaring sirens bounce off nearby skyscrapers, filling the air with a deafening, shrill echo. The sound was mingled with car horns threating other drivers. I watched pigeons pick around garbage cans and saw steam rising up through the vents in the subway.

Then I looked across the street to the temple. It was designed to fit seamlessly into the modern, industrial cityscape that surrounded it. Crisp vertical lines, geometric concrete details, and a quartet of thin, rising stained glass windows gave way to the iconic golden Angel Moroni statue atop a rectangular steeple. As uninterrupted as it looked against the buildings behind it, something about the temple still seemed to detach itself from the city. The peace emanating from it was a stark contrast from the chaotic mess surrounding me. I looked down to assess myself, deemed my work clothes formal enough, and made my way across the street.

In my adult life, I've never opened the front door of any temple without the words "You're gay! You're gay!" screaming inside my head, and this time wasn't any different. It took emotional effort to walk in and make my way through the lobby. At the front desk, a temple worker told me there were multiple young women in the baptistry waiting to be baptized, but only one priesthood holder from my stake had shown up. He was already down there, but they couldn't start performing ordinances until another priesthood holder was there to help. She asked me if I would be willing to serve in the baptistry instead of going through a session like I had planned. I agreed and headed down a set of marble stairs.

It had been quite a while since I'd been to a baptistry. As I descended the staircase I was met with a warm breeze and the faint smell of chlorine. Gold-framed paintings of scriptural baptismal scenes flanked the walls, and a woman in a white dress pointed me toward a heavy mahogany door. I felt comfortable there. It reminded me of that simpler time when I was a youth. I changed into clean white clothes and walked out toward the font. Glass walls surrounded twelve sculpted oxen, positioned in a circle. Resting on their backs was the baptismal font, which sat in the middle of the room. Two semicircular staircases bordered it, one on each side. The room was crowned by a golden chandelier offset by an intricate molding pattern that spanned the ceiling.

I walked through a glass door and passed a long line of young women dressed in dry white jumpsuits. Near the entrance of the font stood the only other priesthood holder who had come to represent our stake. He looked familiar to me, and after a few moments I realized I had met him many months prior, at a stake LGBTQ fireside. His name was Tyran.

He was gay, too.

Tyran, like me, was an NYC transplant. He lived in West Harlem and spent most of his time waiting tables in a diner in Midtown. When he wasn't working, he was painting cityscapes and park scenes. His goal was to become a full-time artist. On the day I met him, he showed me some of his work, and I was taken aback by his ability to capture the movement and energy of the city on canvas.

We spent the evening serving together in the temple—two gay disciples of Christ. We treated each baptism sacredly, taking great care to perform the ordinances exactly as directed. I had walked into the temple with questions, doubts, frustrations, and fears, and I'm sure he had too, but none of that seemed to matter as we served. We understood who we were, where we were, and how special the moment was. It was a scenario I never could have imagined.

One by one, the young women were baptized by proxy, giving souls who had passed on the opportunity to make sacred covenants. The Spirit in the room was palpable. When they had all finished their ordinances, a temple worker took out a stack of blue papers—male family names submitted by the stake—and asked Tyran and me if we would like to be baptized as proxy for those people.

We took turns baptizing one another—holding our arms to the square, praying, and submerging each other into the water. The moment was powerful. When we were finished, we took clean towels and carefully wiped down the area, then I headed back to the changing room and left.

As I walked home I felt gratitude and a considerable portion of awe. I honestly didn't think there was anybody else like me. I thought I was a complete anomaly as far as out, gay men with temple recommends went. But more than that, I was struck by how personal the moment was, and how I felt God watching over me. My identity—my being—seemed to constantly put me at odds with other people in the Church, especially inside the temple. This was the first time being gay had offered me a sacred space where I belonged at church not in spite of who I am but because of it.

I often consider how important this one special moment of belonging was to me. It came at a time when I seriously doubted my ability to stay involved with the Church, just because of how alien I felt compared to everyone else. It showed me I was needed. If I wouldn't have attended, every young woman who had come for stake temple night wouldn't have been able to participate in proxy baptisms. Without me, Tyran wouldn't have been able to serve, either. Plus, instead of having a meaningful, bonding temple experience, he probably would have felt isolated, alone, and a little bit crazy, just as I originally expected to feel. It was validating to find someone who shared a similar background and was working through similar doubts still choosing to be involved. At a time when I most needed it, Tyran helped me feel a sense of belonging.

"Belonging" is a funny term. It seems almost too simple— too remedial—for the powerful feeling it conveys. In a way it's almost paradoxical, for it captures a feeling of oneness with the individual self as well as with a broader group. It is both familial and individual, tribal and all-encompassing. It is a sense of congruence despite all the ways we don't fit in—a state of being where our differences aren't sharp edges or blinking lights, but simply parts of who we are.

Humans have a natural desire for love and belonging. We want to be tethered to others and accepted for who we are.

According to the Interpersonal Theory of Suicide, thwarted belongingness is a direct predictor of suicidal ideation.[12] With this in mind, belonging becomes more than a cute buzzword or an amusing social theory. It becomes a crucial need for human survival. In order to build strong families, strong congregations, and healthy communities, we must foster an environment of love and acceptance so belonging can thrive.

Belonging is a crucial need for human survival.

It's obvious that belonging is important, but how do we create a church environment that includes everyone when there are so many differences among us? I've often reflected on why that one simple experience with Tyran in the temple was able to offer me so much belonging. I believe it was, in large part, due to representation. Tyran was like me, so his very presence offered me space, allowance, and peace. I was able to see part of myself in him and find community and validation in our interaction. To the majority, representation might not seem like much, but to those who feel like certain aspects of themselves don't belong, it can mean the world.

Even if our wards or geographical areas are predominately homogenous, we can increase representation through fostering an environment that allows for diversity, and in turn increase the chances our brothers and sisters at church will feel that they truly belong. In the October 2020 general conference, Elder Quentin L. Cook declared:

---

12 Kimberly A. Van Orden et al., "The Interpersonal Theory of Suicide," *Psychological Review* 117, no. 2 (April 2010): 575–600.

With our all-inclusive doctrine, we can be an oasis of unity and celebrate unity and diversity. Unity and diversity are not opposites. We can achieve greater unity as we foster an atmosphere of inclusion and respect for diversity.[13]

One way to do this is to accept differences and challenges. When we allow others to bring their authentic selves to the table and respect who they are, we signify that we want them to belong. We can simultaneously honor both similarities and differences and make small changes to ensure that everyone feels God's love.

Language can be an especially effective tool to extend belonging and representation to others. I remember always feeling awkward at BYU when business professors would make sweeping comments about "finding a wife" or "making money to support your wife." Straight males in the classroom probably never thought twice about it, but these comments made me (and probably all the women) uncomfortable. They weren't mean things to say, nor were they purposefully isolating, but they still sent an implicit message that people without wives didn't belong in the classroom. During my senior year, however, I had a professor who used inclusive language when talking about dating and marriage. By simply swapping the words "girlfriend" and "wife" with "significant other" and "spouse," she was able to include everyone in the room. Again, I'm not sure the straight males in the classroom even thought twice about it, but for me and many of the women in the class, it helped us feel more welcome.

A shift in language is not the only "small and simple"—but eminently meaningful—way that a sense of belonging can be

---

13 Quentin L. Cook, "Hearts Knit in Righteousness and Unity," *Ensign*, November 2020.

enhanced for all our brothers and sisters. I once met up with a friend who was in town for a family reunion. While eating dinner with his whole extended family, I noticed that they were all shocked when his cousin Nicole walked in. He leaned over and whispered that no one outside of her immediate family had seen her for over ten years. Her reputation in the family was stained with scandal. After her first year of college she had moved in with a girlfriend and left the Church. She was a "long-lost lesbian cousin" who had tattoos and smelled like smoke. Her entrance turned more than a few heads.

To my intrigue, Nicole ended up sitting across from me, my friend, and one of his aunts. She looked uncomfortable as she settled in and started eating her food. After a few minutes of awkward small talk, the aunt asked Nicole about her girlfriend. Nicole choked on her food and dropped her fork. Her eyes began watering and she said, "Thank you for asking. We have been together over a decade and no one in my family has ever asked. You have no idea how much that means to me." The four of us spent the next hour talking with Nicole about her life and ended up spending the whole evening laughing and hanging out together. Nicole found belonging at a family event for the first time in ten years all because her aunt was willing to ask about her life.

We extend belonging to others when we show genuine interest in who they are. No one should feel like an outcast or a burden. People need to be longed for. There's a huge difference between "you can come if you want" and "I want you to come," and it has everything to do with connection and belonging. Consider the power of love without an agenda! What if we stopped treating people like projects? What if we stopped reaching out in hopes that they came back to church, and instead just reached out? What if we stopped seeking to change them, but rather sought to know their hearts? Sister Jean B. Bingham said, "After all is said and done, true ministering is accomplished one by one with love as the motivation. . . . When our hearts are open and willing to love and include, encourage and comfort, the power of our ministering will be irresistible. With love as the motivation, miracles will happen, and we will find ways to bring our 'missing' sisters and brothers into the all-inclusive embrace of the gospel of Jesus Christ."[14]

This kind of genuine, love-motivated interest brought Nicole closer to her family and helped her feel wanted where she hadn't in the past.

It's also important to note that Nicole was an agent of her own belonging. She took those first, courageous steps to show up. The same was true for me at stake temple night. Before I could have that important, healing experience, I had to take a leap of faith and be comfortable with who I was. I had to put myself in a position to belong and do something concrete instead of fantasizing about all the ways I might not fit in.

Too often we go into a situation thinking "Who's going to be my friend?" instead of "Who am I going to be a friend to?" If you go somewhere expecting to not fit in, chances are you probably won't. If you're not confident in yourself or expect to be rejected everywhere you go, it will be much harder to find spaces where you can be your full, authentic self. In this mindset, it's possible to go into a space that's completely, 100% accepting and still feel uncomfortable. Belonging is the intersection of courageous self-acceptance and a Christlike environment.

---

14 Jean B. Bingham, "Ministering as the Savior Does," Everyday Ministering, churchofjesuschrist.org.

Another way to help people belong is to see past the surface. I recently spent a summer working as a therapist at a teen crisis intervention center. I spent eight hours a day working with the most at-risk teenagers in the area. Most of them had serious suicidal ideation, had made multiple suicide attempts, and struggled with self-harm. Others had severe behavioral issues and early onset mental illness. Many had a history of violent acts and drug abuse. They were often dropped off by police officers or sent by schools who could not control their behavior. Almost all of these teenagers were very difficult to work with, and each had very distinct personalities and different presenting issues.

Belonging is the intersection of courageous self-acceptance and a Christlike environment.

There was one client in particular I found incredibly difficult to work with. She had a hateful, disinterested, dark demeanor and caused endless problems with the other kids. She made morbid jokes and had scars all over from getting in fights, which she wore like trophies. She lived at the center for weeks awaiting a far-cry placement with a foster family.

One day we hosted a therapeutic art class with the kids at the center. Surprisingly, and for the first time since I arrived, she participated in the group. She painted a night sky with an alien creature on the moon. She worked hard on her painting and seemed happy with her finished result. Once the art session was over, my supervisor chose her piece to be displayed on the refrigerator. The girl was shocked and said it was the first time her art had ever been displayed on the fridge. Almost immediately, this dark, morbid preteen transformed into a joyful child. She beamed as she went around telling everyone how her painting was chosen for the fridge. To her, having her art displayed in the kitchen at a group home seemed as significant as winning a Nobel Prize.

After this one seemingly insignificant event, the girl changed. She started smiling and pulling her hair back out of her face. She started sharing more and playing card games with the other kids. She also started opening up to me in therapy sessions. I learned her heartbreaking history of trauma and abuse. I discovered she was just a child who had never been loved. Knowing this, I was able to help her build self-confidence and find a sense of belonging. She was never a bad kid. She just needed to feel valued and loved.

If we want to increase the love, safety, and belonging in the world, we need to take people from the fringe and put them on the fridge.

> ## We need to take people from the fringe and put them on the fridge.

The Lord's Apostles have counseled Church members to improve conditions for LGBTQ Saints. Elder Ballard proclaimed, "Certainly, we must do better than we have done in the past so that all members feel they have a spiritual home where their brothers and sisters love them and where they have a place to worship and serve the Lord."[15] Heeding this prophetic call will expand the borders of Zion.

Like me, there are many LGBTQ individuals who love the gospel but don't feel they belong at church. But I believe there's

---

15 M. Russell Ballard, "Questions and Answers," Brigham Young University devotional, November 14, 2017.

a place for us. It will take the sincere effort of covenant Saints to help us see where we fit. Through representation, shifts in language, genuine interest, and acknowledgment, Christlike love can be offered to members of the LGBTQ community. Enacting these changes might take soul-searching effort but will undoubtedly bring unity, restoration, and miracles. Such belonging helped me feel embraced in the temple, reconnected Nicole with her family, and brought miraculous light back to a troubled child of God. These small, simple efforts yielded great results and helped provide others a spiritual home.

Together, we can make belonging *to* the Church of Jesus Christ synonymous with belonging *in* the Church of Jesus Christ, for all of God's children.

7.

LORD, IS IT I?

A S JESUS ADMINISTERED the sacrament to His disciples the night before His Crucifixion, He spoke one of the most uncomfortable phrases in the entire New Testament: "Verily I say unto you, that one of you shall betray me" (Matthew 26:21). I sometimes imagine what it would have been like to be there during the Last Supper. I picture a small room lit by wax candles, the smell of unleavened bread and fresh wine, and a somber yet overwhelmingly spiritual feeling permeating the room. What would it have been like to be a disciple that night? What would I have done if I heard my Master speak those difficult, ill-fitting words?

"One of you shall betray me."

I think my first response would have been to wonder who it would be. I probably would have looked around the room at each of my friends, speculating as to which one of them was unfaithful—which would commit treason. I would probably back up my hypothesis by taking mental calculations of their past mistakes, weaknesses, and all the times they hadn't measured up. I can't imagine wondering if I, myself, would be the one to betray the Savior. After all, I'd be there, dedicating my life to Him and His ministry. And I'd love Him. How could I be the one to betray Him?

That's why I think the Apostles' response is one of the most sincere, valuable acts of humility in scripture. Matthew 26:22 tells us that after hearing the Savior's words, the Apostles "were exceedingly sorrowful, and began every one of them to say unto him, Lord, is it I?" They didn't point to other people across the room and say, "Is it him?" Instead, they looked deep within themselves and asked the poignant, powerful question, "Lord, is it I?"

I am moved by their example. When confronted with a dramatic, unbelievable, uncomfortable scenario, they did not push it away. They did not discredit the allegation, nor doubt any personal responsibility they may have had. They didn't look around for someone less worthy to blame. They did not cut off the possibility that they could very well be the culprit. Instead, they looked deep within themselves. With exceeding sorrow, they exhibited self-reflection and introspection by asking the powerful, heart-wrenching question, "Lord, is it I?"

This question has become a guiding light as I have sought to abandon any intolerance that might exist within me. President Russell M. Nelson recently proclaimed, "Any *abuse* or *prejudice* toward another because of nationality, race, sexual orientation, gender, educational degrees, culture, or other significant identifiers is offensive to our Maker! Such mistreatment causes us to live beneath our stature as His covenant sons and daughters!"[16]

---

16 Russell M. Nelson, "Choices for Eternity," Worldwide Devotional for Young Adults, May 15, 2022.

President Howard W. Hunter also taught the importance of extending love to all. He said, "The pure love of Christ . . . is kind, meek, and lowly" and "has no place for bigotry, hatred, or violence." Instead, "It encourages diverse people to live together in Christian love regardless of religious belief, race, nationality, financial standing, education, or culture." [17]

To follow the prophet, we must identify and overcome our biases.

While serving as a missionary in San Bernardino, California, my companion and I received a phone call from an elderly sister in the ward. She said she recently had two palm trees removed from her yard, but the roots were still out back and made it difficult for her to access her garden. She wondered if we could stop by and remove the roots for our weekly service. We arrived the next day with tennis shoes and gardening gloves, ready to take care of the roots. We scheduled a quick one-hour block for the service, expecting two strapping young men to be able to finish the job in no time. To our surprise, however, once we got around to the backyard, we were met with a task much larger than we'd anticipated.

The palm roots didn't look like any roots I had ever seen before. In fact, they didn't look like roots at all – just unyielding, compact, intricate tangles of mass. Upon inspection, I discovered the roots were as hard as concrete. They were packed tight with rocks, dirt, and sand. We rummaged through an old shed until my companion found a shovel and I had a pickaxe, then spent hours hacking away, dismembering their conglomerate entities little by little. It took an extraordinary amount of effort, leaving blisters all over the palms of my hands. By the time three hours

---

17 Howard W. Hunter, "A More Excellent Way," *Ensign*, May 1992.

were gone, we were completely exhausted and had only managed to loosen up one of the root systems.

Each of us carries opinions and judgments about others that may or may not be true. Our views are shaped by where we are from, the families we grow up in, and the systems we interact with. Painfully, sometimes our views about others based on their identity characteristics do not align with Christlike principles of charity and compassion. These incongruences might be as compact, colossal, and complicated as the roots of a palm tree, but it is up to us to remove any bias that may be inhibiting our ability to access the Lord's vineyard. We could—and perhaps should—spend a lifetime chipping away at those roots.

As I have sought to overcome prejudice toward others, the question "Lord, is it I?" has begun to manifest in a more precise set of questions that provide a useful framework to introspect:

- What implicit biases might I still be holding on to?
- What assumptions do I make about people before I meet them?
- How have the systems I interact with influenced the way I view others?
- Do I stereotype or expect anyone to act a certain way based on their identity?
- Does anything about this person make me uncomfortable, and if so, why?

Part of avoiding abuse and prejudice toward others is prioritizing impact over intentions. Offensive or hurtful comments can seem innocuous when they are well-meaning, but their results can be damaging. If we educate ourselves and seek proximity to those who are different, we can remove disparities between intention and impact. We will realize ways we think we're getting it right but aren't. As a wise refrain says, "It ain't what you don't know that gets you into trouble. It's what you know for sure that just ain't so."

With this in mind, I would like to offer four beliefs/approaches I find unhelpful when interacting with LGBTQ individuals, whether in the Church or otherwise. While the intentions behind them are usually benevolent, I find their impact to frequently be unfavorable. I'll note that the reason I'm including them is because they are quite common. It's likely you've had similar thoughts or used a similar approach in efforts to minister to others. Because of that, some aspects of the next few pages might challenge your viewpoints or make you feel uncomfortable. I invite you to listen to and learn from that discomfort. I pray that as you read my words, you will not discount them, but look for areas to improve while asking, "Lord, is it I?"

1. NOT HONORING WORTH

Viewing gay people as sacred children of God instead of fallen sinners is crucial to helping them see their divine potential. It was incredibly difficult for me to gain a testimony of my eternal identity as a son of God. My struggle to see myself in this simple, most important doctrine was solely because of how I heard others talk about sexual orientation. Being gay is often viewed as a mortal disease, affliction, ailment, or trial. I've heard people compare same-sex attraction to alcoholism, tobacco use, or addiction. It's often pathologized and viewed as a psychological abnormality. This reinforces the idea that gay people are either sinful or damaged, and is intensely harmful to testimonies.

> Viewing gay people as sacred children of God instead of fallen sinners is crucial to helping them see their divine potential.

When I came out, I heard frequent speculation about what made me gay. Some people hypothesized I had been sexually abused or had early exposure to pornography. Others began dissecting my upbringing and trying to assign a "trauma" or "dynamic" that made me attracted to men instead of women. In reality, I had a wonderful childhood. I had loving parents and great relationships with my siblings, and was always involved in extracurricular activities and team sports. Looking for an excuse or reason as to why someone is gay leads to inappropriate judgments that stem from cultural misconceptions. There wasn't a traumatic experience or relationship dynamic that made me gay—it's just how I came into the world.

> There wasn't a traumatic experience or relationship dynamic that made me gay—it's just how I came into the world.

Another cultural misconception is that being gay is all about sex. Before I came out, people viewed me as safe and spiritual. Once people knew I was gay, however, they suddenly saw me through a hypersexualized lens. This disregarded me as a whole person and damaged my view of myself. The pull I feel toward men is not just physical. There are elements of emotional attraction, spiritual attraction, intellectual compatibility, reciprocity, familiarity, romance, and authentic love that all make up my orientation. Understanding this is crucial to overcoming judgment and honoring the humanity of God's gay children.

Being gay is not a choice. It's not something I elect to be or not be, and it's not a defect. It's just part of who I am. I was created intentionally by loving Heavenly Parents, and I believe They know and understand this part of me. Imagine a world where LGBTQ youth know and understand themselves – their individual worth and their divine potential! In order for that to happen, we must throw out cultural misconceptions and see them how God sees them – as beloved, sacred, and good.

2. TRYING TO FIX IT

Sometimes when people learn I'm gay they implement a "fix it" approach by offering ways I could solve the conflict it presents. One of the most common questions I get asked from Latter-day Saints is, "Are you sure you can't just make it work with a woman?" This seems to be the most obvious solution to many people, for it covers the "sin" part of being gay and the "lonely" part of staying single.

What these people don't realize is that asking me to marry someone of the opposite sex is similar to me asking them to marry someone of the same sex. If you identify as straight, I invite you to think about a friend who is your same gender. Think about how much you care about them and all of the fun you have. Now, close your eyes and imagine dating them. Imagine having a big wedding, being intimate, and raising children together. What sorts of feelings arise when I offer that scenario? Do you feel offended? Are you repulsed? Whatever you feel, it's probably similar to how I feel about marrying a woman. This suggestion also rarely considers the partner's point of view, or recognizes that *they* would be married to someone who isn't romantically, emotionally, or sexually oriented toward *them*. I have dear friends who have chosen this path. I love and support them, but let's recognize that it's not for everyone.

Other people suggest I stay single until I die and that God will work things out in the end. They compare that option to single straight members of the Church, not stopping to realize the glaring difference: hope for marriage in the future (*or* in the next life). They often bring up other single Saints, saying things like, "See, he's doing it! That means you can do it too!" What they often don't realize is that coming out but staying single doesn't just come at the cost of companionship and meaningful connection, it still limits Church participation. There are callings, leadership roles, and temple covenants that are not offered to single Saints. We belong to a very marriage-focused church, and celibacy doesn't lead to eternal marriage.

All in all, I've found that suggestions for my life, whether they be to stay single, marry a woman, or even leave the church and marry a man aren't helpful. Being gay is not something to solve. If anything, it's something to learn about so we can all become better disciples of Christ. Instead of trying to fix someone, I recommend having a sincere conversation. Ask them about their life experience, what values guide their choices, and how you can best support them. I'm confident this approach will heal division and lead to increased enlightenment and understanding.

> Instead of trying to fix someone,
> I recommend having a
> sincere conversation.

3. MAINTAINING DOUBLE STANDARDS

I often see differences in how people are viewed and discussed based on their orientation. Within Church culture, an entirely separate vernacular has been created for talking about gay vs. straight individuals. When straight people date and fall in love, we say "they dated and fell in love." When gay people date and fall in love, we say "they acted on their homosexual feelings and are pursuing a same-sex romantic relationship." When straight people are attracted to the opposite sex, they are "people." When gay people are attracted to the same sex, they are "people who experience same-sex attraction." I've never heard anyone ever talk about "heterosexual tendencies," the "straight lifestyle," or "the straight agenda" but those phrases flood conversations where gay people are discussed.

Words have the power to either unify or divide, and when people use an entirely different vocabulary to talk about gay people, that creates a divide. To me, it indicates the person talking is uncomfortable with my existence or thinks the way I experience love and attraction is somehow different than how they do. If everyone applied the same dating, marriage, and relationship terms to all people, regardless of identity, it would help close the social hierarchy between people based on orientation.

Another disparity I see is how people view same-sex couples as loud, garish, and obtrusive. I recently wrote this kitschy poem to poke fun at the double standard:

> *Wedding invites in the mail*
> *Your fridge their destined place*
> *But if one was from two men you'd say*
> *"Quit shoving it in my face!"*

Sometimes gay couples are accused of being "in your face" for doing the same things heterosexual couples do without thought or question. If you feel offended by seeing two women holding hands at the mall, but don't bat an eye when a straight couple starts massaging each other's backs during sacrament meeting, there might be something to look at there!

4. EXPRESSIONS OF CONDITIONAL LOVE

I often find well-meaning people who cling to phrases and ideas that aren't actually helpful when ministering to LGBTQ Saints. One phrase I commonly hear people say is, "It's okay to be gay as long as you don't act on it." I've noticed most people really like this approach because it feels like a way to show acceptance while maintaining the Church standard of chastity. It seems like an easy, clean-cut way to manage the complexities of sexual orientation as they relate to religion.

However, to be honest, I know very few gay people who feel comforted by, or even remotely connected to, that phrase. For many, it feels like a misrepresentation of what orientation is and how it manifests in their lives. I once had a friend jokingly say, "What do they mean by 'acting on it'? Is listening to pop music and watching chick flicks 'acting on it'? Because I do that all the time, and I don't plan to stop!"

As silly as it was, I think my friend made a really good point. The term "acting on feelings" is incredibly vague and doesn't correlate well to the lived experience of many gay people. For me, being gay is an integral part of who I am. My orientation isn't a room in a house I can keep locked up so I don't go in. It's more like the type of lumber used to frame the house. It's integrated into the entire structure. My orientation isn't "feelings," it's an orientation. It influences my relationships, my testimony, my interests, and how I see the world. When I am my authentic self, I am acting in accordance with my orientation, and that makes me feel happier and closer to God.

Another issue I find with this particular phrase that it carries a message of "I love you, but . . ." We live in a world where LGBTQ youth are almost five times as likely to attempt suicide compared to heterosexual peers.[18] They constantly face a barrage of messages that tell them their identity is gross, wrong, sinful, and embarrassing. In many cases, this one, vulnerable aspect of their being has received nothing but hate, deprivation, and shame since the day they first discovered it.

I myself spent years worrying my orientation would separate me from my family, my faith, and everything I loved. When I finally mustered up the courage to come out to my mom, she said, "I love you. I always have, and I always will. Whatever you choose and wherever your life takes you, I want to be part of it." I found her sentiment much more powerful than if she would have said, "I'm okay if you're gay as long as you don't act on it." Her expression of unconditional love healed parts of my soul I didn't even know were broken. It is that type of message that will save our LGBTQ youth.

I find that many people are terrified of a more accepting approach because they don't want to be responsible for giving someone else permission to sin. They want to uphold their values and ensure those values are shared so others can experience the happiness they have. The problem is, if you are worried about showing too much love or constantly trying not to condone sin,

---

18 Michelle M. Johns et al., "Trends in Violence Victimization and Suicide Risk by Sexual Identity among High School Students—Youth Risk Behavior Survey, United States, 2015-2019," Morbidity and Mortality Weekly Report, Centers for Disease Control (August 21, 2020): 19-27.

you are never truly able to sit with someone and understand their experience. I have found that a much more powerful, Christ-centered approach is to honor agency and give God's LGBTQ children unfailing love, the same way my mom did to me. I believe this will lead to healthier individuals, stronger testimonies, and more unified families. It's unproductive to sit around worrying about whether we are condoning sin when people around us are contemplating taking their lives.

> **If you are worried about showing too much love or constantly trying not to condone sin, you are never truly able to sit with someone and understand their experience.**

But what if someone does act on it, in the way that is . . . you know . . . actually acting on it? What if someone decides to date, marry, or have sexual relations with someone of the same sex? How do we interact? How do we show love? How do we support them while also supporting Church teachings?

My advice comes directly from chapter 3: Invite them to Dinner.

Even if just metaphorically, the best thing to do is share your food. Learn about them and appreciate their goodness. Meet their partner and introduce them to your own. Go to their wedding and invite them to your baptisms. Welcome them to your weekend barbecues and go to their midday brunch. Make your home a place where they feel embraced and loved.

I've found that, even if we don't agree, people are going to do what they are going to do. We can't choose how someone exercises their agency. That's part of God's plan. We can choose, however, how involved we want to be in their lives. If we exile gay couples from our inner circles, we miss out on some of God's finest, most introspective, most creative children. I promise you, associating with LGBTQ people from different walks of life will help you grow and more fully understand the Savior.

* * *

It can be difficult to make adjustments for others, and more difficult still to challenge old ways. The humility required to consider if you're part of "the problem" is herculean. But this approach strengthens Zion and cultivates stronger families and communities. Without asking, "Lord, is it I?" or seeking feedback on how to improve, it's possible to impede others and not even know it.

A few years ago I was assigned to a work project in Tunis, the capital of Tunisia. On my last day in the city, I decided to take a few hours off and visit the beach. I hailed a taxicab and rode past palm trees, ruins, mosques, and stray goats until the Mediterranean opened up before me. I ran down the beach and right into the clear blue-green waters. It was a paradise, the horizon stretching as far as my eyes could see.

After swimming for a bit and cooling off, I started making my way down the shoreline. Before long, I came across a group of teenagers doing tricks off a mound they had fashioned from sandbags. They ran across the hot sand, launched themselves off their makeshift ramp, and flipped their bodies through the air. They reminded me of my dunk team friends from college.

I stood there for a while, gawking at how talented they were. I could tell they didn't have any formal training, but their air awareness and athleticism amazed me.

Before long I started feeling like I was missing out. I made my way over to introduce myself. They looked puzzled, unsure as to why a grown foreigner would approach them. I realized they didn't speak English, so I gestured to their setup and started making flipping motions with my hands. One of them muttered something in Arabic to his friends, then looked to me and said, "Sorry. Sorry." The whole group turned around and started walking back toward the road.

"Wait!" I called after them, humored that they thought I was asking them to leave. "No!"

They turned back around and I did the only thing I knew would break the communication barrier: a standing backflip. They threw their hands in the air, whooping and hollering with the recognition of what I had been trying to say—I didn't want them to leave, I wanted them to let me join!

We spent the rest of the afternoon flipping on the beach under the hot North African sun. They demonstrated which angles were best for hitting the pile of sandbags and showed me how to land so I wouldn't thud too hard if I didn't make it all the way around. Once we were into it, we almost didn't need words. The shared experience of being gymnasts was more than enough. They taught me how to position my body better when I twisted, and I showed them how to push through their shoulders and snap their legs down for faster back handsprings. The combination of their street knowledge and my technical training gave us all something to learn.

As golden hour approached, one of my new friends ran to grab a camcorder. He gave instructions in Arabic to his friends, who subsequently arranged themselves in order. One by one, they showed me his vision. I was to jump off the pile of sand, flip over someone in a handstand split beneath me, and step out into a roundoff connected to a series of handsprings that ended in a full twisting layout. As I hit the ramp and did my handsprings, the others would flip both over and through me, creating one seamless train of acrobatics. If it worked, it would be incredible.

We each practiced our parts a few times, then assembled for the video. Once I got the thumbs up, I ran as fast as I could, vaulted off the sandbags, and soared over the handstand. *Perfect*, I thought as I split my legs and continued my tumbling series. I landed my last element flawlessly, then looked to see everyone else. To my surprise, most of them had fallen. They laid strewn in the sand, looking disappointed.

"It's all right!" I nodded encouragingly. "Let's do it again!"

Over and over we attempted our trick combination, and over and over they fell. I started to get agitated. I was hitting my part ninety percent of the time, working as hard as I could, but they kept falling repeatedly. The only other person to get it right was the guy in the handstand, and he wasn't even doing anything! The others talked amongst themselves, gesturing to me, and pointing out the path I was supposed to run.

Yes. I thought. *It's fine. I'll keep going until you guys can get it right.*

But I was starting to get tired. I didn't understand why they weren't as good anymore. Was it the pressure of the camera? Were they just not trying as hard? Communication was a barrier again. I had no idea what was happening.

I realized that, in all the excitement, I forgot I had a phone with internet access. I ran to my bag, pulled it out, and opened a translation app. "What is happening?" I translated to Arabic. "Why does everyone keep falling?"

I handed my phone to their lead tricker, and he started typing away. The translation came back in broken English: "Your timing very difficult. Please, if you can, run slow, and flip more fast. We cannot make our flip."

I suddenly felt like a complete fool. It all made total sense! I was almost a foot taller than most of them, and had much longer legs. With the timing of my approach, and the length of my flip, they couldn't cross through me without hitting me in the air. They were each adjusting to *me*, and in doing so, were unable to land their own tricks. I had been judging them for messing up, but in reality, they were sacrificing themselves so I wouldn't get hurt. I hadn't even considered that I might be the problem.

I felt terrible for judging them, and worse for all the times they'd hit the sand at my expense. I wished I had asked for feedback sooner. I repeated the only English word I knew they were familiar with, "Sorry!" And practiced my part again with their corrections in mind. The new timing made it more difficult for me, but I was still able to get around.

After I'd adjusted, the camcorder switched on, and we attempted our performance once again. This time, it was flawless. They sailed through the air, flipping and twisting around me as I tumbled across the beach. We all finished at the same time, our bodies landing upright and strong in the sand. We pumped our fists in the air, cheering and running toward each other to celebrate. They slapped me on the back and gave me fist bumps as we made our way over to watch the video. It was as if I'd never messed them up at all.

Just as my tumbling approach kept throwing off my Tunisian friends, the cultural approaches used in the Church often throw off LGBTQ Saints and cause them to fall in the sand. When their worth is diminished and their orientations reduced to sex, they can't clearly recognize their divine potential. If people around them suggest "solutions" to being gay, they'll feel abnormal and defective. When they confront divisive language and double standards, they'll likely feel "othered" from the fold, and if the messaging they hear has undertones of "I love you, but . . ." they will never truly feel loved.

> **The cultural approaches used in the Church often throw off LGBTQ Saints and cause them to fall in the sand.**

By contrast, seeking genuine feedback and making small adjustments can help them land on their feet and bring them closer to Christ. This might mean putting forth extra effort to "correct our timing," but doing so will undoubtedly lead to collective success. Purposeful introspection allows us to let go of cultural misconceptions that impede others and creates an environment where everyone can thrive. Through recognizing personal accountability, prioritizing impact over intentions, and heeding prophetic counsel to root out bias, we can expand Zion's borders to include God's LGBTQ children.

May we each follow the example of Christ's humble Apostles by suspending judgment and asking the invaluable, transformative question:

"Lord, is it I?"

8.

THE ADVOCATE

M Y LITTLE BROTHER SAM got tossed around quite a bit on his mission. After completing training at the Mexico City Missionary Training Center and serving for about a year in Bolivia, he was emergency evacuated from his area due to political unrest. From there, he was moved to the Sao Paulo Brazil MTC while he awaited reassignment and visa documentation. After a long month of limbo he made it to a new mission in Colombia and finally hit his stride. He was elated, but the normalcy was short-lived when he, like so many others, was sent home early due to the COVID-19 pandemic.

Sam had kept a bright and optimistic faith all throughout his chaotic missionary experience, but returning home early was difficult for him. He went from baptizing on the beautiful beaches of Cartagena, Colombia, to a mandatory quarantine in "middle-of-nowhere" Missouri. I made it home to Missouri just a few days before he did, escaping the disorder in New York City and taking refuge in my little hometown. Life abruptly went from international flights and skyscrapers to hay bales and county roads.

Like most people during the pandemic, Sam and I had no idea what to do. We were grateful for the extra time we had to spend with family, but we felt like our lives had been ripped away from us. Things started to feel pretty heavy as we worried for the world, for our futures, and for loved ones who were sick. Ultimately, that heaviness (and if I'm being honest, a great deal of boredom) led us to go on a cross-country road trip to shake ourselves from the monotony.

Our final destination was Salt Lake City, but we decided to take the long way to get there. Our great-grandparents had once lived in a small town in west Texas, so we started there on a family history tour. We found our ancestors' gravestones and were able to locate the house where my great-grandpa was born. As we continued our trip, we stopped at lookout points and went sightseeing in places we had never been before. This led us through southern New Mexico to hike desert mountains and up to Santa Fe to visit historical churches and landmarks. The points of interest made for a memorable trip, but the most meaningful part was spending time together.

There was one conversation, in particular, that will stay with me forever.

A few hundred miles east of Albuquerque, Sam told a story that led to an unexpected debate. He began sharing about a man he had met on his mission named Rogelio. Rogelio came from an overlooked tribal group in Bolivia and spoke a lesser-known dialect. Because of his background, he was deemed undesirable by society. Sam recounted how he had worked with leaders in the ward to reach out to Rogelio even though he was different. Rogelio ended up finding a friend who spoke his dialect and was willing to translate at church. Over the course of a few months, he became an integral part of the ward, leading service projects and working with youth. He was eventually baptized and found joy and community for the first time in his life. At his baptism, Rogelio cried with gratitude and thanked his ward members for how accepting and helpful they had been.

As Sam told the story, I was torn. I loved hearing how the humble ward was willing to accept a stranger and take him in as their own. I loved how they didn't care that Rogelio spoke a different language or came from a background most in society frowned upon. It was amazing to hear how congregational acceptance helped him receive the gospel and turn his life around. At the same time, I felt sensitive to the fact that Rogelio was accepted at church despite having a different identity, but many people like me were not. Just weeks before, I had talked with a friend who had been removed from his ward calling after coming out as gay. He was fully active and worthy of a temple recommend, but his local leaders were uncomfortable with his identity and didn't trust him to teach Sunday School lessons. I wanted everyone's experience to be like Rogelio's, but it seemed like whether or not a ward was willing to accept an outcast directly depended on what kind of outcast a person was.

As Sam finished his story, I shared some of these complex thoughts. I expected them to lead to a discussion about how to help everyone belong at church, but Sam was not happy with my critique.

"Seriously, you're really going to be like that? Why do you always have to be so negative about the Church?" he said, surprising me with his sudden reaction to my comments.

"Be like what? I'm not trying to be negative. I'm just being realistic. For every one person who fits, there is another who doesn't. Until we can fix that, I feel like it's important to bring up."

"You're always complaining about how there's no place for gay people, but that's not true. You fit just fine. Heck, you wrote a book about it. I'm not saying it's easy, but sometimes you've just gotta buck up."

"Are you kidding?" I bit back. "I've never fit 'just fine.' That's *why* I wrote the book, Sam. Every time I go to church I have to put myself in a position to get hurt just to take the sacrament. I buck up all the time. It's the only way I can survive. But I don't know how anyone can honestly expect LGBTQ people to stick around if nothing changes. And that's the thing, most don't stick around. Do you realize how hard it is? And nobody ever seems to care."

"That's so dramatic, Charlie. We grew up in the same church with the same leaders. You act like everyone's always trying to hurt you, but you know that's not true. You can't let this anger get in the way of your testimony. You know the gospel is true."

"I know. I love the gospel. That's why I want things to be better. Just because people aren't *trying* to hurt me doesn't mean they never do."

"Well just stop focusing on it so much. It's making you create a problem that's not there."

"The problem is there, Sam. Maybe you just can't see it because it doesn't affect you."

Sam rolled his eyes and shook his head. "Stop playing the victim."

My face dropped. "Never mind," I said quietly. "It's not worth it. I won't bring it up anymore."

We drove in silence.

A few awkward minutes later Sam broke the tension.

"I'm sorry. I don't want to fight," he said. "I guess felt a little attacked and I let my emotions get the best of me."

"Thanks. It's okay," I said. "I'm sorry too. I don't want you to feel attacked. This has never been an easy topic, and probably never will be."

"Can we open the conversation back up?" he asked. "I want to hear what you have to say."

"Really?" I ventured.

"Yeah. I really do. I've been gone a long time. I want to know what things are like for you."

"Thanks . . ." I began. "I really do love the Church, Sam. I'm devoted to it. It's made me who I am. And you're right, much of my experience has been positive. I have been treated wonderfully by Church leaders. I have an incredibly supportive family and amazing friends. I have every privilege that could possibly be given to a gay Latter-day Saint . . . and it's still so, so incredibly hard. I get passionate about this because I think, if it's this hard for me, what is it like for everyone else?"

"That makes sense," he said. "What about it has been hard lately?"

"I try but I can never be completely comfortable at church. I'm always on my guard. I never know when someone will say something offensive about people like me. I never know when Church teachings will be used against me. My stomach flips when I think about how quickly policies shift and how they have affected me in the past. It all feels so volatile. I can never truly be at peace. I'm not trying to complain, and I really don't think anyone is ever trying to hurt me, but that doesn't mean it doesn't hurt."

"That sounds exhausting," Sam admitted.

"It is. And it's true, Sam. Even though we grew up in the same church with the same leaders, we haven't had the same experience. When you sit in on a lesson about eternal marriage and exaltation, you envision yourself in the temple with a wife. I sit there and feel like a freakish outsider. Each time the Family Proclamation is brought up, you think about how wonderful it will be to have a family of your own. I brace for a comment about the evils of being gay. Even general conference is hard. Every six months I sit down with a notebook and a pen and pray I don't get blindsided."

"Dang. That's rough," said Sam.

"Yeah. That's just how it is though. It's so weird to be so consistently hurt by people I love so much. It makes me question things sometimes, you know? I have to really focus on the gospel basics in order to hold on."

Sam thought for a moment.

"Well, when you're a bishop you can make sure nobody in your ward ever feels that way."

"Sam, that's the thing—I'm never going to be a bishop. I'm gay, remember?"

The realization slowly dawned on his face. Priesthood leadership positions were only held by men with wives.

Sam opened his mouth a few more times, then subsequently closed it. He looked wholly defeated. He tried to hide it from me, but I saw tears begin to well up in his eyes. I knew he was feeling some of the frustration that too often characterized my membership in the Church. Technically, I had won the argument, but there was no victory in it. We sat in quiet sorrow beneath the weight of the conversation.

After a few moments, to my surprise, Sam again broke the silence.

"Then, if *I'm* a bishop *I* will make sure nobody in *my* ward ever feels that way," he replied in a much different tone. He was no longer defensive or defeated, but profoundly resolute. The words weren't just full of compassion and love, they were charged with electric determination and earnest resolve. There was nothing performative about his promise. In this display of perfect allyship, discipleship, and empathy, Sam modeled what I had never been able to put into words.

I have contemplated the arc of that conversation over and over again. It began with a disagreement over whether my critique was valid. To Sam, it seemed like I was complaining about a problem that didn't exist. My experience was so far out of his frame of reference that he wasn't able to relate to it. This made me feel overlooked and him feel defensive. Sam's defensiveness increased when I noted that my orientation posed challenges his did not. It was a hard thing to hear, and probably felt accusatory.

At this point, the conversation could have easily turned sour. Sam could have kept disregarding my viewpoint and maintaining his position that everything was fine. He could have discounted my experience and held his ground after telling me to stop victimizing myself. He could have reprimanded me for criticizing something he held dear. He could have told me to simply get over it or spouted off reasons why church was hard for him too. There are a million ways he could have deflected the conversation or disregarded my feelings, and he almost went down that path.

But he didn't.

Instead, Sam chose empathy. In an incredible display of Christlike love, he resisted the urge to react defensively and made space for what I was saying. Even though he'd never felt anything like it, Sam chose to believe my lived experience. He asked me questions, took my words at face value, and practiced humility as he sought to recognize hard truths within them. Then, Sam defied human nature. He acknowledged our disparity and made a conscious decision to use his position to help. He promised to spend his time, his energy, and his influence to help solve a problem he would never have to deal with himself.

He found the root of Christlike charity.

It's a huge sacrifice to change how you live to make room for someone else. It seems unnecessary to inconvenience oneself to solve a problem that has never affected you. Additionally, it's awkward and uncomfortable to consider that you might have inherent cultural advantages based on an identity or characteristic you can't control. But I believe that's where Jesus lives. In that tumultuous, sensitive, taxing space were humility, empathy, and charity collide, we become true disciples of Christ. As we selflessly consecrate what we have to lift and empower others, we put off the natural man and fulfill our most sacred covenants as disciples of Christ.

When Jesus bled in the garden and hung on the cross, He displayed the single greatest act of empathy in history. As an all-powerful being—Creator and God of the universe—Christ willingly offered Himself for the powerless. His Atonement was love and sacrifice in their purest forms. Imagine the humility required to seek, understand, feel, suffer, and die for the pain of someone else. Without recompense or obligation, Christ willingly subjected Himself to drink the bitter cup as He used His power to break the shackles that bound humanity. To me, it is no wonder that Christ is known as the "Advocate." His concern for the vulnerable and voiceless is unparalleled and evident in everything He does.

As Latter-day Saints, we exemplify the Savior when we do the same. Part of our covenant to take Christ's name upon us means taking on the role of advocate. We each have power and influence we can use to support and protect others. This is done by giving voice to the voiceless and taking stewardship over inequality. Like my brother Sam discovered, it often includes inconveniencing oneself to alleviate the cause of someone else's pain. This is not only selfless and admirable; it is the essence of Christ's Atonement, and the root of covenant faith.

> **Part of our covenant to take Christ's name upon us means taking on the role of advocate.**

I think sometimes it's easy to get into a "why does it matter?" mindset. If we are all children of God, it seems that where someone is from, what color their skin is, or how they identify should all be inconsequential. It might even seem like using such identifiers is a way to breed division among us. But I think that's kind of the whole point. In a perfect world, everyone would be seen without labels and treated as equals. Everyone's opportunity, access, and happiness would be directly proportional to their work ethic, obedience, and faithfulness.

But in this fallen world, that's rarely the case.

Identities matter when they influence how people are viewed and treated. In this probationary state, race, gender identity, ethnicity, physical ability, and orientation are often a source of inequality among us. They impact opportunities, resources, privileges, and influence. They help determine where we live, what positions we are able to hold, and how we are viewed by others. It may seem overwhelming to think of all the ways we differ from one another, but this doesn't have to be a bad thing. We can use these differences to teach us essential lessons and become more like the Savior.

Identities matter when they influence how people are viewed and treated.

Those who feel portions of their identity put them at a disadvantage can learn resilience and self-confidence as they work through challenges. The tension their identity provides can be used to develop patience, learn forgiveness, and build community with others. They can learn to work hard and have faith as they seek to decrease any gaps in opportunity they may encounter. I have seen this firsthand as a gay member of the Church. Because my religious experience is coupled with increased complexity that stems from my orientation, it has pushed me to be a more engaged believer. Feeling marginalized by my orientation has been my driving force to seek Jesus Christ. It requires me to constantly exercise my faith and helps me look for the good in difficult situations.

In a similar manner, those whose have identity traits that belong to a majority can use their position to develop Christlike characteristics. They grow in humility and charity as they recognize inequalities around them and seek for ways to empower others. They become more selfless as they leverage their influence to uplift and advocate for those around them. They overcome pride as they "seek not for power, but to pull it down" (Alma 60:36). They foster the expansion of Zion as they lend their voice to those who historically have not had one, as Sam promised to do for me.

As we acknowledge, accept, and honor our differences, they can become meaningful and meaningless at the same time. I see this clearly with my brother. To him, me being gay simultaneously means everything and nothing at all. He honors my orientation as he works to support me and overcome misconceptions. He protects and defends me when others belittle or devalue this aspect of me. He works to make space for other LGBTQ individuals and uses his influence to lift and love them. He goes out of his way to do all of this because I am gay. At the same time, Sam doesn't see me as my orientation, he just sees me as me. I'm not his gay brother, I'm just his brother. At the end of the day, I am just Charlie, and he is just Sam. Our identities influence the way we interact and how we serve each other, but we are bound by a much stronger, shared identity that is infinitely more important. We are brothers, covenant keepers, disciples of Christ, and children of God.

As Saints, we can achieve this same unity when we seek to overcome prejudice and become sensitive to feedback from minorities. If anyone feels marginalized or held back by an identity characteristic they cannot control, we have failed as a faith community. We cannot afford to shut them down and assume everything is fine. The prophet Nephi taught the danger of such complacency when it comes to Zion. He foretold the adversary would work to make Saints comfortable and content with how things are. 2 Nephi 28:21 says, "And others will he pacify, and lull them away into carnal security, that they will say: All is well in Zion; yea, Zion prospereth, all is well—and thus the devil cheateth their souls, and leadeth them away carefully down to hell."

> If anyone feels marginalized
> or held back by an identity
> characteristic they cannot
> control, we have failed as a
> faith community.

For many identities, including LGBTQ Saints, all is not well in Zion. Many feel they have to present a watered-down version of themselves in order to fit in. Others are unable to find belonging altogether or are subject to harsh criticism and hurtful misconceptions each time they go to church. In these cases, the reason people make their identity such a big deal is because it is. Due to how they are viewed and treated, their worship is invariably connected to pain. I dream of a world where their cries are not discounted or diminished, but used as signifier of where the Saints can improve.

Moroni spoke of the charity it takes to unify the Saints and become true disciples of Christ. He wrote, "And charity suffereth long, and is kind, and envieth not, and is not puffed up, seeketh not her own, is not easily provoked, thinketh no evil, and rejoiceth not in iniquity but rejoiceth in the truth, beareth all things, believeth all things, hopeth all things, endureth all things. Wherefore, my beloved brethren, if ye have not charity, ye are nothing, for charity never faileth. Wherefore, cleave unto charity, which is the greatest of all, for all things must fail—But charity is the pure love of Christ, and it endureth forever; and whoso is found possessed of it at the last day, it shall be well with him" (Moroni 7:45–47).

As covenant disciples of Christ, let us do everything we can to ensure our congregations are holy spheres where everyone can belong. Like my brother Sam, let's offer charity to those who feel hurt, marginalized, or misunderstood. Like our Savior, let's take the time to visit each individual identity, problem, and pain, then make sacrifices to uplift and empower the vulnerable. Let us "succor the weak, lift up the hands that hang down, and strengthen the feeble knees" (D&C 81:5). As we do, I have faith that our differing identities will no longer be stumbling blocks, but tools that help us become united in our shared identity as children of God.

We become disciples of Christ when we become advocates, like Him.

9.

COVENANT ALLIES

A FEW SUMMERS BACK, I went on a group camping trip and drove there with my friend Haley. We were super excited to have a relaxing weekend getaway and just be able to spend time in nature. On the drive to the campsite we jammed out to throwback songs from our high school days and caught each other up on our busy lives. We spent the first afternoon pitching our tents and setting up camp, then started getting to know the other campers. It was a big group, with friends of friends we hadn't met before. Then we spent the next few days hiking through a national forest, kayaking on the lake, and staying up late into the night roasting marshmallows and telling stories.

As fun as it was, there was one part of the weekend that didn't sit well with me. At one point during a hike, I overheard two of the people in our camping party voice some offensive opinions about gay people. As I listened to them talking, I realized they didn't know I was gay. In most circumstances I would have

stepped in and defended myself as part of the LGBTQ community, but I was caught completely off-guard. Furthermore, I felt
exhausted. I had wanted this weekend to be free from anything
related to advocacy or me being gay. I knew if I spoke up, I
would probably hear more hurtful things and have to practice
a lot of grace and patience. I didn't have the energy for that
conversation, so for the sake of trying to take a break and be on
vacation, I begrudgingly let the comments slide.

I mentioned this to Haley on the drive home, and was surprised to find she'd had a similar experience. One of the campers had cornered her and asked intrusive questions about her
ethnicity, skin color, and the texture of her hair. They brought
up derogatory misconceptions about Black women and made
jokes about whether or not she fit those stereotypes. Haley said
she was really upset by the comments but ultimately decided
not to address them. She didn't have the energy to educate the
other campers on how hurtful they were. Instead, she removed
herself so she wouldn't have to endure the conversation.

We were both upset as we shared our stories with each other.
Haley was mad that I had overheard homophobic comments,
and I was furious that she had encountered racism. We were
both a little frustrated at ourselves for not shutting down the
problematic comments we heard, but more than anything we
were annoyed that our self-care came at the cost of perpetuating
bias. In order to salvage our vacation and not deplete ourselves,
we had to let multiple people maintain hurtful beliefs without
any pushback.

As unfair as it might seem, this is often the burden of minority groups. Those who are exhausted from feeling marginalized,
hurt, and misunderstood are often the same ones who have to
spend extra energy to correct other people's misconceptions. If

someone doesn't have that energy, like when Haley and I were on our camping trip, the offending person carries their beliefs forward to potentially marginalize and hurt someone else.

I've spent a lot of time thinking about that camping trip and how to solve that peculiar aspect of minority stress that leads people to feel burnt out, alone, and overwhelmed. One thing I've found helpful is to have educated allies who are willing to step up and carry some of that burden. I didn't have the energy to address any LGBTQ issues, but I absolutely had energy to step in for Haley. She felt the same way about me. While she was exhausted by the thought of correcting racially insensitive jokes, she would have shut down the campers' negative remarks about gay people without a second thought. Both of us had the capacity to step in and bear each other's burdens, even though we didn't have capacity to carry our own.

> **Both of us had the capacity to step in and bear each other's burdens, even though we didn't have capacity to carry our own.**

In Mosiah chapter 18, Alma taught about the sacred covenants made through baptism. He said, "As ye are desirous to come into the fold of God, and to be called his people, and are willing to bear one another's burdens, that they may be light; Yea, and are willing to mourn with those that mourn, and comfort those that stand in need of comfort, and to stand as witnesses of God at all times and in all things , and in all places that ye may be in . . . if this be the desire of your hearts, what have ye against being baptized[?]" (Mosiah 18:8–10).

I'm often asked by members of the Church how they can be allies to LGBTQ individuals. I think the best way to do this, when you boil it down, is to understand and keep baptismal covenants. If every member of the Church earnestly sought to mourn with those that mourn, comfort those who stand in need of comfort, and bear one another's burdens, we could unify divisions and heal so much of the pain that exists in the world.

The first step in bearing another's burdens is knowing what they are. It's important to be well educated in order to be an effective ally. This often includes listening to stories, challenging personal assumptions, and acknowledging people's expressions of sorrow, pain, or discomfort. People with different identities have unique burdens, so we need to listen to them and learn how we can help.

> ## The first step in bearing another's burdens is knowing what they are.

One burden many LGBTQ people carry is the weight of "what if?" and a fear of rejection. During the summer of 2012, I had an unlikely best friend in a middle-aged cake decorator named Lisa. I was eighteen years old, and in order to earn money for my mission I took a job as Lisa's assistant at the local bakery. I had some basic skills and a lot of natural talent, but Lisa's ability was next-level. She was a wizard with a piping bag, effortlessly trimming cakes of all sizes in fresh buttercream icing. She taught me tricks of the trade, and before long we could take care of a stack of cake orders faster than anyone in Southwest Missouri.

Lisa was very backwoods. She always wore dark blue jeans and a hat from the local feed and grain store. Usually around people like her, I watered down my real personality and tried to put on a much more masculine front. But as we got to know each other I got more and more comfortable being myself. We had a mutual love for country music and found an old FM radio that we plugged into the bakery counter. We sang along to familiar George Strait songs, talked about our lives, and drew out daring wedding cake designs to attempt.

One day a young man came to the bakery to sell supplies. I noticed him immediately, even before he walked through the door. I caught myself staring as he entered and introduced himself as the new sales rep. He smiled at me with big, bright eyes and asked how I was doing. I squeaked out a quick, "I'm fine, thanks." Lisa cocked her head to the side and shot me a quick glance, then took out an order sheet and started going over business with him.

Every now and then the new sales rep would lift his eyes and look my way. My gut twisted. I felt excited, confused, twitterpated, and completely sick. I was terrified by how attractive he was, and I had a strange feeling he was interested in me, too.

In a desperate, terrified rush, I ran to the back freezer to "take inventory." I stayed there as long as possible, shivering in the big, icy box. I started beating myself up internally, shrouding myself with thoughts like, "You're disgusting. What's wrong with you? Future missionaries aren't supposed to have feelings like this." I knelt down in the freezer and said the thousandth prayer for God to change me. Somehow, this situation seemed especially dire. There was a real person behind my attraction. I was terrified by the thought of liking someone who might like me back.

"What's up?" asked Lisa when I finally came out of the freezer, some thirty minutes later.

"Nothing," I choked. "Just thought I would check inventory and organize some of the stuff piling up back there."

"Oh. Thanks! I'm sure that'll help things run more smoothly. Plus you know I get cold in there," Lisa said with a laugh.

I moved a finished cake section off of my turntable and replaced it with two carefully stacked eight-inch rounds. George crooned in the background.

"You know, my uncle is gay," Lisa said nonchalantly as I filled my piping bag with buttercream.

"Huh?" I stammered, almost dropping my spatula.

"My uncle. He's gay. He's my favorite uncle, too. He had a really hard time coming out. His parents didn't take it well. But I support him completely. I'm really proud of him."

"Oh . . . well . . . that's really cool of you," I said awkwardly.

"Gay people are just people, you know? That's what I believe."

"Yeah . . . yeah, totally."

We worked in silence for a bit.

"I see you hide sometimes when people from school come in to get groceries," Lisa continued. "Like you're afraid of what they will think of you?"

I kept working, smoothing icing onto the eight-inch rounds.

"You don't need to be embarrassed of anything. You are one of the most creative people I know. If they make fun of you for that, shame on them."

Ten years later, it's interesting to think back on that interaction. At the time, there's no way I would have considered myself gay. Though it maybe should have been obvious, the word wasn't even in my vocabulary. It took me years beyond that moment to accept this part of who I am and stop shaming myself for it. However, I never forgot that conversation with Lisa.

After I came out publicly, some of my "what if?" fears came true. There were important people in my life who started treating me differently. Some were very curt, and others unfollowed me on social media. I confronted misunderstandings, awkward moments, and people talking about me behind my back. But there was one person I never worried about—a backwoods, hat-wearing, cake decorator named Lisa. By actively expressing love and support, she removed my fear of rejection long before I even knew how much I needed it.

Elder Dale G. Renlund taught, "As we develop faith in Jesus Christ, we should also strive to become like Him. We then approach others with compassion and try to alleviate unfairness where we find it; we can try to make things right within our sphere of influence." He further stated that "not throwing stones is the first step in treating others with compassion. The second step is to try to catch stones thrown by others."[19] In short, we move forward on the covenant path when we carry people's burdens and intercept stones aimed at them.

> **We move forward on the covenant path when we carry people's burdens and intercept stones aimed at them.**

Sometimes, when proverbial stones are hurled my way, people try to convince me they don't hurt. It's not uncommon for me to hear phrases like, "Why do you always have to talk about your sexuality?" "Why don't you just let it be?" "Why do gay people always make things such a big deal?" But instead of telling others

---

19 Dale G. Renlund, "Infuriating Unfairness," *Liahona*, May 2021.

which stones should hurt and which ones shouldn't, a higher approach is to believe them, and to catch those stones.

As I was completing my master's program at BYU, there was an address given that resulted in considerable pain for me and many other LGBTQ students. In the aftermath, a division between certain Church members and people within the LGBTQ community surfaced more deeply than I had ever seen before. The result was a very "us vs. them" scenario that left me and many others completely dumbfounded.

Over the course of the next few days, my social media became a war zone. I felt like I was being pelted with stones. Messages like, "If you don't like it, you can leave" crowded my feed, and many members of the Church, in efforts to defend their faith, posted incredibly insensitive comments. For me, it was like something straight out of a nightmare. As a public figure in the Latter-day Saint/LGBTQ space, I even feared for my physical safety. I remember that week as one of the worst of my life. I watched the covenant people of my church mock and disregard the pain of their LGBTQ brothers and sisters, and I also saw members of the LGBTQ community mock and belittle members of my church. As someone who occupies a middle ground, I felt unwelcome, unwanted, and misunderstood on all sides.

A week after the incident I was still messed up. I had not been sleeping well, and my emotional reserve was completely depleted from ministering to friends who were struggling with unsupportive family members. As I was doing my best to plow through the pain, I received a text from Whitney, a friend and mentor who worked as a diversity and inclusion liaison in BYU's athletic department. The text began with a thoughtful paragraph about how much she appreciated me and the perspective I brought to the university, followed by a list of times she had available in her schedule. She said if I needed to process, rant, or just sit with someone who cares, I could swing by any time.

I took her up on the offer that same afternoon. I went to her office, sat down on her couch, and shared my frustrations. I expressed the confusion I felt and how heavy the week had been. I had a list on my phone with everything that upset me about the situation. I went through it one by one, expressing deep frustration that nobody seemed to care how many people were hurting. I told her about the stones that were thrown my way and how much it hurt that nobody was there to intercept them.

Even though the damage had already been done, Whitney offered herself as someone to help heal that pain. She allowed me to share my honest thoughts without feeling judged. When I was angry, Whitney let me be angry. When I was hurt, she let me be hurt. She didn't diminish any of my emotions or my reactions. She didn't worry about my testimony or try to defend the Church. Instead, she listened, internalized, and empathized with me. For the first time in a long time, I felt like I didn't have to package everything perfectly in order to be heard. I raised my voice, contradicted myself, and jumped between topics. All the while, Whitney was neither defensive nor put off. She asked clarifying questions, validated my experiences, and took sorrow in my suffering.

As I mourned, Whitney mourned with me.

I've pretty much accepted pain to be a consistent part of my Church experience. As long as I can remember, I've felt whiplashed by changing policies, shifts in language, and contradictory opinions. To some, that might seem foreign, but for many gay Latter-day Saints, it's just part of the burden we carry. While under the weight of that burden, it seldom helps when people preach to me, give me advice, or tell me to "just get over it." I feel bolstered by those who help me feel valued, seen, and understood. People like Whitney give me the strength I need to carry on.

Sometimes, intercepting stones might mean removing perceived judgment. I recently set up an appointment with my stake presidency to renew my temple recommend. As I was waiting in the hallway, I started to feel anxious and sick to my stomach. I found it strange, considering I had already passed through the first interview round with my bishop and I knew I was worthy to enter the temple. I'd even heard from multiple sources that my stake president was supportive of other gay members in the stake.

But that didn't do much to make my nervousness go away. I realized that, due to a lifetime of trying to figure out where I fit in the Church and plenty of not-so-lovely experiences, my body was bracing for impact. The idea of having an interview with a Church leader I didn't know made me apprehensive and on edge.

Our conversation began with small talk about where I grew up and what I'd been up to lately. While we talked, I couldn't shake the unpleasant feeling. Then, before the interview portion, my stake president told me he was grateful for the chance to meet with me and thrilled to have me in the stake. He said he had been trying his best to listen to and learn from LGBTQ Saints, and asked me to let him know if I saw any areas where the stake could improve. He expressed a sincere desire to do anything in his sphere of influence to help me and other LGBTQ members of the stake feel welcomed at church.

Even though there was never any threat, I was still nervous before the interview. But, because my stake president went out of his way to express his appreciation and support for me, he was able to remove my fears and help me feel more at ease. He recognized the burden I carried and actively intercepted it. As Elder Jeffrey R. Holland taught, "We may not be able to alter the journey, but we can make sure no one walks it alone. Surely that is what it means to bear one another's burdens—they *are* burdens. And who knows when or if they will be lifted in mortality? But we can walk together and share the load. We can lift our brothers and sisters as Jesus Christ lifted us."[20] Acknowledging challenges LGBTQ members of the Church face and actively seeking to share their load draws everyone nearer to the Savior.

My camping trip with Haley taught me firsthand the importance of allies. We couldn't bear the burdens that stemmed from our own identities, but we had the ability and energy to help each other. That's the power of effective allyship. Someone who is educated, aware, and proactive can make a huge difference. They can identify and catch stones, and minimize and reverse pain. It may not even take some grand, heroic effort. In my life, some of the best allies were a cake decorator who removed my fear of rejection, a school administrator who mourned with me while hurting, and a Church leader who took active steps to mitigate my anxiety. Each of these people was attuned to the burdens I faced because of my identity and went out of their way to help bear them. As we seek to establish Zion, we must do the same. Allyship is achieved when we keep our baptismal covenants and bear one another's burdens.

---

20 Jeffrey R. Holland, "Bearing One Another's Burdens," *Ensign*, June 2018.

10.

SUPPORT AT EVERY STAGE

STILL REMEMBER WHEN my friend Jessy landed her dream job as a high school seminary teacher. We had lunch together to celebrate, and while we were eating she stumped me with a question I'd never been asked before. "I'm sure I'll have LGBTQ youth in my classes," she said. "I really want them to feel safe and supported, but how do I know what approach to use? It seems like everyone has different experiences, different comfort levels, and uses different terminology. And even then, people's needs are always changing! I'm not sure how I'll keep up!"

I spouted off something like, "If you're not sure what someone needs, you can usually just ask!" But I knew it wasn't a very good answer. She had an excellent point—every LGBTQ individual is always at a different place on their journey. There are countless factors that impact how someone views their orientation, and knowing how to help can be tricky. I thought about her question often, and couldn't give her a solid answer until much later.

While working as a therapist at BYU, I was introduced to the Cass Model of Identity Development, a research-based framework published by Dr. Vivienne Cass. The model consists of six stages of LGBT identity development, informally known as the "six stages of coming out." It was created after studying a large sample of LGBT individuals and documenting how they changed over time. The first three stages are internally focused, meaning the individual's primary challenge is coming to grips with their orientation. The final three are outwardly focused, when they are trying to figure out how they fit in society.[21]

While not every LGBTQ person follows this model exactly, learning about the stages of coming out helped me answer Jessy's question. They provide a helpful guide for understanding what someone might be going through and the support they might need. Throughout this chapter I will explain the stages of coming out, how I've typically seen them manifest in gay Latter-day Saints, and what members of the Church can do to provide support throughout the process. I pray this information helps you develop greater empathy and recognize where you can be a more effective minister to God's LGBTQ children.

STAGE ONE: IDENTITY CONFUSION

The first stage of coming out is Identity Confusion. Within this stage, a person starts to feel a sense of incongruence. They feel different from their peers and become initially aware of possible attraction to the same-sex. The realization they might not be heterosexual is often marked by curiosity, confusion,

---

21 It's important to note that, while the stages are sequential, a person's life path can vary. It's common for individuals to loop or revisit stages throughout their lives.

and conflict. This usually coincides with the most formative, vulnerable years of childhood and adolescence.

For my friend Devin, this stage began at a very young age. As early as three years old he remembered feeling different from other boys around him. He recalled playing house and wanting to be the mom every time so he could pretend to have a husband. He played with his sister's dolls, wore his mom's high heels, and felt most comfortable around girls. He remembered being drawn to men both in real life and on TV, but at such a young age never stopped to think why. As a child, he didn't view whatever was different about him as a bad thing—it was just the way he was.

Devin said the realization that he was attracted to men came when he was about twelve, right when his body started going through puberty. While most adolescents his age had innocent crushes that brought butterflies and giggles, Devin's first crush barraged him with shame. He had just been ordained as a deacon and recalled feeling disgusted with himself while passing the sacrament the following Sunday. Devin felt like God must hate him, and that Heavenly Father wouldn't want such a disappointing son to carry the bread and water to the congregation.

To cope with the stress and confusion he felt, Devin slipped into a state of denial that would last through most of his adolescence. Whenever he thought a guy was attractive, he told himself it was because of jealousy or admiration. On the flipside, when he thought a girl was cool and fashionable, he repeatedly told himself it was a crush. His denial helped him manage the shame he felt. He wasn't ready to deal with the consequences of admitting he was attracted to men. But even in his denial, Devin's orientation remained constant. He began having nightmares of being thrust to hell and separated from his family. He worried his existence was at odds with God's plan. He fasted and prayed that he wouldn't be gay. From the outside, he appeared like a healthy, active, high-achieving preteen, but behind his facade he felt depressed and alone.

As Devin continued his teenage years, he began researching ways to "cure" himself of same-sex attraction. He showed me a faint scar beneath the inside of his palm from snapping a rubber band each time he saw a man he was attracted to. He thought, if he associated attractive men with physical pain, he would overcome the feelings that haunted him. He began externalizing and redirecting his self-hatred toward other gay people. He used homophobic slurs and avoided anything that might be viewed as gay.

Without a healthy outlet to figure out his sexuality, Devin's shame and curiosity led him to pornography. He used it first to "test" if he was really attracted to men, and later as a coping mechanism for the shame that shrouded his life. He associated his orientation only with sex, and his unwanted pornography use increased the shame and self-hatred he felt, ultimately creating a dependent cycle. In time, Devin started pulling away emotionally from his family and regularly wishing he were dead. He said it seemed like a more palatable option than being gay, and an escape from the seclusion and pain he felt.

Devin's story of confusion, shame, isolation, and unhealthy coping is very common for people in the first stage of coming out. For many gay members of the Church, this stage spans years—sometimes even decades—and is marked by spiritual, emotional, and psychological trauma. To make matters worse, this stage is usually kept completely secret. It is often the longest, most damaging time period of someone's life, but they never tell anyone what's going on behind the scenes.

For someone looking to provide support, this secrecy poses a problem. It's likely you will never know when someone is in this stage. They'll struggle in silence, living in denial and internalizing every message they hear about sexuality and orientation. In order to help, it's imperative to treat every church and family interaction as if there is a gay person in the room. Let people catch you being kind to LGBTQ individuals. Ask yourself what message you might be sending to any closeted people in your life. Those in the Identity Confusion stage need to be constantly reminded they are loved, wanted, and valuable. They need to know there is nothing they could ever be or do that would pull them away from the love of their Heavenly Parents.

> ## Let people catch you being kind to LGBTQ individuals.

STAGE TWO: IDENTITY COMPARISON

The second stage of the Cass model is Identity Comparison. In this stage, a person begins to accept the possibility of being predominately attracted to the same sex. They become more and more aware of how different they are from heterosexual peers and feel alienated from those around them. They grieve the loss of the life they thought they would have, namely a future involving marriage and children, and many feel jealous of heterosexual couples. At this stage it's also common for LGBTQ people to engage in same-sex romantic behaviors, but deem it as normal expressions of friendship. They compartmentalize their actions and do everything they can to maintain a heterosexual identity.

When I met Laura, a student who came to me for therapy, she was still working through much of the shame and unhealthy coping that marks the first stage of coming out, but was no longer actively trying to convince herself she wasn't attracted to women. Her orientation wasn't a reality she *wanted* to accept but rather something she felt obligated to "deal with." Like many in this stage, Laura shuddered at the word "gay." She only felt comfortable using the phrase "experiencing same-sex attraction." That language felt far less threatening, as it indicated orientation was something happening to her, not part of who she was. She viewed it as a temporal challenge that would be healed at the resurrection. She often quoted scriptures like Ether 12:27 and "endure to the end."

When I asked Laura if anyone else knew about her same-sex attraction, she told me she had confessed to her bishop. I asked her what she confessed—to my knowledge she hadn't done anything to warrant a trip the Bishop's office. She worked at the MTC, served as Relief Society president, and spent her free time baking cookies for ward members. Laura took a few moments to think before replying, then said, "I guess nothing, really. It's just that who I am feels like a sin."

It broke my heart that Laura believed her very existence was offensive to God.

Laura told me she'd given up hope that her same-sex attraction would go away but wanted to learn how to manage it so she could get married in the temple. She regularly went on dates with guys but never felt interested in any of them. She felt jealous of how easy it seemed for everyone else to find love and envied "normal" women.

As I talked more with Laura, she frequently contradicted herself. Her attitude shifted from "I know this is my cross to bear" to "I wish I could be with a woman" to "I'm a disgusting freak." She saw her same-sex attraction as a barrier to future happiness and grieved the life she thought she would have. Accepting her orientation felt like killing her future, and ripped her away from hope of temple marriage. Sometimes Laura would have panic attacks that sent her back into thought processes typical of the previous Identity Confusion stage. Laura was very uncomfortable with her orientation and felt incredibly isolated and alone.

I think the worst thing I could have done for Laura would have been to give her advice. When someone is tangled and hurting, the natural human response is to step in and try to fix their problems. I've found, however, that people in the Identity Comparison stage just need to feel loved. They already feel crazy enough—they don't need someone to tell them they don't make sense. They need the security and refuge of being with someone who sits in their pain, grieves with them, and gives space for their conflicting thoughts and emotions.

STAGE THREE: IDENTITY TOLERANCE

In the third stage of the coming-out model, Identity Tolerance, a person starts to admit they are probably gay. They start looking to see if there's anyone else like them, and are astonished to discover there is. It's common for someone in this stage to try on various labels to find what feels most congruent with how they feel. As they meet and interact with other gay individuals, they are often forced to confront their own internalized homophobia.

I suppose I entered this stage the first time I said the words "I'm gay" out loud. I tried the label on as if it were a pair of jeans. It was a word I had always been terrified of—like Laura, I had always figured if I said I was gay, it would envelop my whole life and put me on a path to destruction. However, something about viewing my orientation as an unchanging part of who I am was incredibly healing. Moving away from the term "same-sex attraction" helped me stop viewing my orientation as something exclusively sexual. The term "gay" felt more representative of the aspects of my orientation that go beyond physical attraction. I started feeling happier and closer to God.

In order to start piecing together a new future, I wanted to meet other people like me. I started reading blog posts from other gay members of the Church and looking at social media pages of Latter-day Saint/LGBTQ support groups. I was astounded by how much their stories felt like my story. One day, as I was scouring Facebook for resources, I saw that Paulette, a girl from my YSA ward, had "liked" one of the posts. It took me by surprise—until then, it all seemed like a separate world. I didn't realize there were people I knew who were part of it. In a moment of bravery, I decided to reach out. I sent Paulette a cryptic message saying I wanted to meet up and talk.

A few days later I met up with Paulette at a picnic table outside her apartment complex. I soon came to the realization that I didn't know her well at all, and I felt awkward as I beat around the bush with meaningless small talk. I stalled as long as I could until she finally asked me point blank why I wanted to talk.

"Oh. Yeah. Well, um. I saw this Facebook post you liked."

I described the post to her.

"And I was just wondering what your connection is, and why you liked it."

"Oh," she replied, caught somewhat off-guard. "Well, I think it's cool that there are organizations helping gay members of the Church find community. I guess I don't really have a connection, I just thought it was interesting, so I liked it."

"Oh," I said stupidly. "So you support gay people."

"Yeah. I mean, why would I not?"

It quickly dawned on me that I was about to tell someone I was gay. But not just someone— someone I knew. Someone who I interacted with every week and who had access to almost all of my friends. I needed to be sure I trusted her, so I started playing devil's advocate.

"Don't you think it's gross though?"

"What? Of course not," she replied sternly. "I—"

"And what about the Church? How can you say you're a member if you support people being gay?"

I bombarded Paulette with questions, testing her knowledge and her protectiveness over my secret. Finally, she'd had enough.

"Look, I'm not sure why you wanted to talk to me about this, but I'm not going to sit here and let you say horrible things about children of God. I doubt you have any idea how damaging your opinions are, and I guess you're entitled to them, but I won't spend another minute listening."

She huffed and started getting up from the table.

"Paulette, wait," I said.

I paused for a long moment.

"I . . . I'm gay."

Realization dawned on her face. She understood what I was doing and why I had been so callous.

I blurted my feelings. I told her how confused I felt and how scared I was. I told her she was the only one in the entire state who knew, and I had no idea what I was doing. Paulette listened with misty eyes and encouraging nods.

"Oh, Charlie. I'm so sorry. Thanks so much for telling me," she said when I finished ranting. "What can I do to support you?"

I told her about an off-campus support group I desperately wanted to go to. I wanted to meet other gay people who were college-age and were raised in the Church. I still wasn't ready for anyone to know I was gay, but I needed the community and connection that came from being with people like me.

"Okay. Well what if go with you? We don't have to tell anyone who we are, and we can be super low-key."

"You would do that for me?" I asked earnestly.

"Of course!"

"But what if people think you're lesbian? Doesn't that bother you?

"Not at all. I don't think it's embarrassing to be gay. And I don't think it's *gross* either," she said with a wink.

"Want to know something funny?" Paulette said as we got up from the table. "All my roommates and I were *convinced* you were coming over to ask me on a date!"

"As long as the 'date' is the gay support group, I'm in!" I said with a laugh.

The next week Paulette took me to the support group. I stayed quiet the whole time, but simply being present in a room with other gay members of the Church still brought healing beyond compare. It normalized my experience and helped me find a community I never knew existed. Paulette continued to accompany me until I was confident enough to go on my own. Her support was unparalleled.

Gay individuals in the Identity Tolerance stage need people like Paulette—caring friends who allow them to awkwardly unscramble their orientation without judgment. They often need support and community but either don't know how to find it or are too timid to reach out. By being comfortable in the space and willing to walk alongside a struggling LGBTQ person, you could make all the difference.

> **Gay individuals need caring friends who allow them to awkwardly unscramble their orientation without judgement.**

STAGE FOUR: IDENTITY ACCEPTANCE

The fourth stage in the Cass development model is Identity Acceptance. This is the first externally focused stage of coming out, where someone usually begins to disclose their orientation with social groups. In other words, people in this stage begin coming out on a broader level. They shed childhood shame as they seek more social interaction with gay individuals, and they sometimes start dating. At this stage, many experience the "gay adolescence." They face a learning curve as they confront the adult world without the developmental milestones afforded to most straight individuals during their teenage years. People who have felt rejected by heterosexual friends and family often try very hard to fit in with any new gay people they meet. This sometimes results in actions that go contrary to their values and beliefs and can stir up anger, sadness, and grief.

At the Identity Acceptance stage, my heart started smiling for the first time. My internal dialogue changed from "You're revolting," "You're hopeless," to "You're all right," "You'll get through this." I finally felt okay with who I was and more hopeful about the future. Coming out to friends and family helped me feel congruent with how I was perceived and who I actually was. I found greater support and stronger community, and felt closer to people I loved most.

I vividly remember the first time I made a joke about being gay. I was on a road trip with my cousin and the navigation system said, "Continue *straight* for ten-point-two miles" in its robotic female voice. I bit back, exclaiming, "No thanks, Siri, I already did that for twenty-three years!" My cousin burst into laughter, and my heart burst into joy. Admittedly, it was low-hanging fruit, but bringing up my orientation without the usual heaps of pressure and dread was unbelievably liberating. I felt weightless and free.

While the sparkle and hope of Identity Acceptance can be transformative, the "gay adolescence" aspect of this stage can pose unique challenges, and sometimes even danger. While I working as a therapist at BYU, I met a clean-cut sophomore named Mason. Mason told me that a few weeks prior, in efforts to find someone to talk to, he had created a profile on an anonymous dating app. In his late-night moment of depression and despair, he messaged strangers until one of them replied. They started messaging regularly, and Mason shared his fears of being a gay BYU student who had recently returned home from a mission. Mason said messaging the stranger gave him hope and made him feel normal for the first time in his life.

Eventually, the man wanted to meet in person, but Mason was terrified of being seen in public. He decided it would be safer to go for a late-night drive to avoid any unexpected social interactions. Mason was apprehensive but excited to meet up. Deep in the canyon, they sat in a car and talked for a few hours. Mason felt like he was unlocking a part of himself he had always kept hidden. As the time passed, Mason's date started making physical advances. They were welcomed at first, but Mason soon felt uncomfortable and overwhelmed. Mason said his insides began screaming. He didn't know how to say no and stand up for himself. He'd never had to hold a boundary before. Instead, he froze completely.

Mason returned home traumatized. The next day was Sunday, but he didn't go to church. He felt disgusted with himself and too ashamed to be in God's house. He spent the whole day in bed, spiraling in depression and self-loathing. He stopped eating, avoided friends, and missed class for the whole rest of the week. He blamed himself for what had happened to him.

In this stage of coming out, safety is essential. Mason's story is neither uncommon nor unique. Like many gay Latter-day Saints, Mason never had the formative, coming-of-age experiences that lead to healthy relationship decisions as an adult. He didn't start by going on group dates at sixteen. He never openly talked about crushes. He didn't involve his parents, hold hands before kissing, or learn how to set and uphold physical boundaries. His first "date" with someone he was attracted to was accidental, in a dark, parked car with an extremely uneven power dynamic.

I imagine how much different things would have been if Mason had had someone there for support as he confronted the gay adolescence. Instead of looking to a stranger for advice, what if his mom, a Church leader, or a friend could have been trusted? If he ever did end up going on a real first date, what if he had felt comfortable meeting up in public or in a group setting? What if he'd had someone to help unpack the experience? What if, at the very least, he could have told someone where he would be, who he'd be with, and when he'd be home?

One supportive, nonjudgmental person could have saved Mason from trauma, loneliness, and sexual assault.

In this stage, many gay members of the Church end up in some form of same-sex relationship. Those without supportive friends and families often do it in secret. This leads to late nights, closed doors, and locked cars. Many grow up hearing their orientation is a sinful, shameful, secret, so as adults they treat it as such. If they don't have the space to operate in the light, they won't. They'll feel forced to places where people they know will never find them—bars, clubs, or different cities. They'll venture out into the world, grown adults with the dating experience of high school freshmen. This can put naïve, inexperienced people in incredibly overwhelming, isolating, and dangerous situations. If they get taken advantage of, or even make honest mistakes, many feel they are irreparable and pull away from God.

Because this is the first externally facing stage of coming out, this is often where being an ally makes religious people feel conflicted. They start asking themselves questions like, "Can I support this? Am I condoning sin?" Indeed, many Latter-day Saints feel comfortable offering love and support to gay individuals who hate themselves and are ashamed of who they are. But once they accept themselves or feel any amount of pride, Church members often feel nervous and pull away. I believe this is the absolute worst thing you can do. The gay adolescence, combined with a distant or unsupportive family, is a recipe for danger. Mason's story is mild compared to others I know. The need for communication and support during this stage is more crucial than I could ever describe. For gay loved ones to be safe, they have to feel comfortable living in the light.

> The gay adolescence, combined with a distant or unsupportive family, is a recipe for danger.

STAGE FIVE: IDENTITY PRIDE

The fifth stage of coming out, Identity Pride, is ushered in by feeling an intense need to publicize individuality. A person in this stage wants everyone to know their orientation and will brandish their identity. They often put distance between themselves and those outside the LGBTQ community, and emphatically associate with all things "gay." Many view the societal separation of gay and straight as "us vs. them" and feel sour toward anyone who fits the heterosexual norm. This stage is frequently paired with a rejection of institutions associated with past shame and an impetuous desire for activism.

A few years ago my sister Hannah and I did a month-long "Murph" workout challenge with our dad. The challenge, named after a fallen military veteran, consisted of one hundred pull-ups, two hundred push-ups, and three hundred body squats, bookended by two separate one-mile sprints. To make things more difficult (and solely to test our self-discipline) Hannah put us on a strict diet. For the duration of the challenge she proposed we not eat any sugar, carbs, or processed foods.

Every day for a whole month we woke up before sunrise to complete a "Murph." No matter the weather, we pushed our sore muscles and blistered palms through the workout. Over time, our bodies grew stronger, and we started completing the Murph faster and faster each day. The diet part of the challenge, however, seemed to get worse as we went. The longer I went without my nightly pint of ice cream, the more I craved it.

On day thirty, we threw a celebration. We made reservations at our favorite restaurant and ordered whatever we wanted. My dad controlled himself, but Hannah and I did not. We overcorrected and ate more dessert than a whole ward potluck combined. Every ounce of self-discipline went right out the window the moment our self-imposed food restrictions were gone. That night, both of us got sick. The sugar rush was a shock to the system.

During the Identity Pride phase of the coming-out model, this same phenomenon tends to happen to gay individuals. After countless, difficult years of lying, running from ourselves, and hiding our identities, we overcorrect. We gorge ourselves on our newfound self-acceptance, often resulting in an overidentification with being gay. While this can sometimes pose problems, for many, this stage is essential. It allows us to overcome the shame and chagrin of every prior stage. Sometimes, as LGBTQ individuals rapidly shed their shame, it might appear like they're shedding some of their decency as well. The shift can seem sudden and unexpected to friends and family, leaving them shocked by the rapid change in persona. In most cases, those who feel supported will recalibrate in time.

For me, this stage manifested in a rejection of heteronormativity. As soon as I received my undergraduate degree from BYU, I bleached my hair and moved to New York City. I bought a clip-on ear cuff (I never could get myself to actually pierce it) and wore bolder patterns and tighter clothes. I wanted new people I met to immediately know I was gay. If that was going to be an issue, I didn't want to deal with them. I was so sick of having to come out and worry who might reject me. I started embodying gay stereotypes I had always tried to avoid. Letting go of my shame felt addicting. I wanted to immerse myself in queerness, so I purposely sought out gay friends and followed gay celebrities on social media.

Simultaneously, I felt a sudden interest in LGBTQ history. I read accounts from the civil rights movement, educated myself on the AIDS epidemic, and learned about court rulings regarding same-sex marriage. There was so much I didn't know about my LGBTQ predecessors, and I drank in the information. The more I learned, the more I felt a desperate need to advocate. I felt angry at the social mistreatment of LGBTQ individuals, both in the past and in the present.

By all accounts, this "intense pride" phase of my life wasn't all that intense, and it lasted a little over a year. Throughout it, I kept strong relations with friends and family. They were exceptionally supportive of me and showed interest in what I was learning. Their encouragement helped ground me and maintain myself while confronting Identity Pride. Their support allowed me to hold my same interests, beliefs, and personality, even with my sudden, fierce association with the mainstream gay image.

My friend Aiden, however, had a different experience. When he entered this stage of coming out, he received pushback. As he experimented with his style and started going public with his orientation, his dad met him with sharp opposition. He told Aiden nobody cared about his sexuality and that he needed to "just shut up about it." He expressed disgust when he saw Aiden post photos with a rainbow flag and said he was embarrassed his son was becoming "one of those loud, flamboyant gays."

Aiden countered his dad's reaction by pushing further into identity pride. He felt angered by the way he was treated and stopped going home to visit. He surrounded himself exclusively with other LGBTQ people and referred to them as his "chosen family." In line with the Cass model, he started rejecting "heterosexual values and institutions." The pain and sorrow he felt at the intersection of faith and identity converted to anger and vitriol. His internal dialogue moved from "I'm bad, I'm wrong, I'm toxic," to "straight people are bad, society is wrong, the Church is toxic." Aiden removed his records from the Church, started frequenting clubs and parties, and built an entirely new social life in line with mainstream gay culture.

Identity Pride is important because it helps LGBTQ people overcome shame, but it's usually a little messy. The surefire way to lock someone into a destructive version of this stage is to shame and dismiss them while they're in it. People here need patience and support. The chief difference in my Identity Pride phase compared to Aiden's was the way our families reacted. Because my loved ones were patient and expressed unabashed interest in my life, I could take the positive aspects of Identity Pride and move forward to the next step. Aiden, however, could not. He had to find "chosen family" because his own family didn't choose him. This caused him to take Identity Pride to haphazard extremes, and he was never able to mature out of the stage in a safe, healthy way. Just like me and my sister after the Murph, Aiden kept eating too much sugar, and he kept getting sick.[22]

STAGE SIX: IDENTITY SYNTHESIS

The sixth and final stage of the Cass model is Identity Synthesis. It is marked by the discovery of a "new normal." In this stage,

22   It should be recognized that the Identity Pride stage differs from Pride month, which is typically celebrated in June to commemorate the birth of the LGBTQ civil rights movement in the United States. When some people think of Pride, they picture city-wide parades featuring scantily clad men. While it's true that you may see clothing and behavior that appears "loud" and "in your face," Pride isn't just a parade. Most cities also sponsor interfaith worship services, community art nights, service projects, mental health initiatives, and suicide prevention efforts. Events are attended by all sorts of people across the LGBTQIA+ spectrum, as well as friends and allies. The celebrations certainly have elements typical of Stage 5 in the Cass Model, but Pride month isn't just about protest and visibility. It's about building community, celebrating progress, overcoming shame, and eliminating prejudice and discrimination.

being gay becomes less of an identity and more of an aspect of self. A person no longer views their orientation as a categorizing label, but just as part of who they are. They integrate themselves into all parts of society, both gay and straight, and don't define "sides" based on orientation. Many continue involvement in public advocacy, but with less brazenness and vitriol. Anger toward past shame or oppression decreases in intensity and can be directed in healthier ways. A person in Identity Synthesis feels comfortable with who they are and settles into their own place in society.

Identity Synthesis is very hard to achieve for gay members of The Church of Jesus Christ of Latter-day Saints. To be honest, most leave the Church before they even get to this stage. Those who do stick around usually don't feel synthesis, but instead discover continued challenge. The predominant Latter-day Saint and LGBTQ cultures both hold that being gay and being religious are mutually exclusive. These conflicting cultures make people feel pinched between the two. They are never able to settle into their own place in society, because there isn't one.

For me, being a public figure at the intersection of faith and sexuality consistently puts me in the crosshairs. I am met with relentless pushback from LGBTQ individuals who have left the Church. Many get locked into the Identity Pride stage, and they project their rejection of "heterosexual institutions" onto my life. They berate me for still going to church. To them, I cannot truly be gay, or even an ally, unless I renounce my faith. This pressure is draining, and results in me feeling unsupported and alone.

On the flipside, because I'm confident in my orientation, members of the Church are often afraid of me. They worry associating with me or listening to my experiences will cause people to lose their testimonies. Some even still think being gay is a lifestyle choice and worry that any acceptance might influence their children—or even turn them gay. They seem to wish I had stayed at stage one or two, because that would be more comfortable for them. Those who aren't overtly offended by my orientation are still usually unsure what to do with me. They can't figure out how I fit in the plan of salvation, and they feel awkward thinking about it. When I'm at church, my orientation can't just be a seamless part of who I am, because it sticks out like a sore thumb. The Church of Jesus Christ of Latter-day Saints is not a comfortable place when you're gay.

Even though I feel congruent in who I am and what I believe, it's still hard to achieve true identity synthesis. I consistently feel like I'm too gay for the Church and too churchy for the gays. The two communities I feel I most belong to both reject me. I'm not sure which one hurts worse.

In order to help LGBTQ members of the Church achieve synthesis, we have to change the cultures that prohibit it. We can no longer be complacent with a world where LGBTQ people feel like they have to reject the Church in order to accept themselves. We need to expand the borders of Zion to provide a middle ground for those who feel torn by their concurrent, unalterable identities as gay children of God. As Elder Renlund said, we must "fully mirror Christ's love and love one another so openly and so completely that no one feels abandoned, alone, or hopeless."[23]

> We can no longer be complacent with a world where LGBTQ people feel like they have to

---

23 Dale G. Renlund, "Our Good Shepherd," *Ensign*, May 2017.

reject the Church in order to accept themselves.

Understanding how to better support LGBTQ individuals will relieve pressure on both sides of the "Identity Synthesis Pinch." On the Church side, it will foster an inclusive environment where gay individuals can find a spiritual home. It will keep them safe, healthy, and buoyed up as they attend their local congregations. On the LGBTQ side, it will help individuals mature through destructive aspects of the Identity Pride phase, thus reducing the contempt they aim at those who still associate with the Church. Offering Christlike charity to all LGBTQ individuals gives those who seek to stay in the Church more space to breathe and a greater chance of achieving identity synthesis.

* * *

In Matthew 13, Christ gave the parable of the sower, telling the story of seeds that were planted in different ground. He taught, "Some fell upon stony places, where they had not much earth." Those seeds weren't able to take root, because they weren't on fertile soil. When they began to emerge, the sun scorched them because they couldn't draw water or nutrients. There were other seeds that "fell among thorns; and the thorns sprung up, and choked them." Because of their menacing surroundings, those seeds were never able to grow. Instead, they suffocated and died. A third set of seeds, however, "fell into good ground, and brought forth fruit, some an hundredfold, some sixtyfold, some thirtyfold" (Matthew 13:5, 7–8). These seeds were planted in fertile soil and had nurturing environments that allowed them to thrive. Because of this, they could fully mature and provide delicious fruit.

As my friend Jessy noted in her seminary class, different people need different support at different times. Though this may seem overwhelming, understanding the stages of identity development can help determine what each individual needs and when. With that support, LGBTQ youth will be able to grow and mature through each stage on fertile ground, safe from the unforgiving rocks and smothering thorns that would otherwise inhibit their growth. By providing healthy, encouraging environments for God's gay children, we can keep them safe as they navigate the complexities of coming out, and we can create nurturing environments where they can prosper and be fruitful.[24]

---

24 Vivienne Cass, "Homosexual Identity Formation: A Theoretical Model," Journal of Homosexuality 4, no. 3 (1979): 219-35.

11.

WHERE ARE THE SAMARITANS?

I WAS ON MY MISSION when the Church published a website called Mormon and Gay. It was a game-changer for many gay members of the Church. The website featured stories of faithful Latter-day Saints who identified as gay, lesbian, or same-sex attracted. They each bore testimony of the gospel and shared inspiring stories of how they were finding peace at the intersection of faith and orientation. A few of them were in mixed-orientation marriages, but the majority were planning to remain single for life.

I visited the website week after week during family email time on my mission. I would open it in a hidden browser in a separate tab to make sure no other missionaries saw what I was doing. I slowly chipped away at the stories, reading in quick flashes while my companion and district-mates were distracted with emails. To me, the people highlighted on the website were a lifeline. They were the first representation I had ever encountered of others like me. I saw myself in their stories. I found a new vocabulary—one that explained how I felt and how I experienced the world. Their stories gave me hope.

It was astonishing to visit an official Church website and see Latter-day Saints who acknowledged their orientation while still holding on to their faith. The idea that someone could say they were gay and be a member of the Church was astounding. As a solitary wanderer grasping in the dark, realizing there was someone else like me was a light. I linked myself to these strangers. I internalized their stories and used them to fortify my own. They became my inspiration as I navigated the treacherous waters of reconciling faith and orientation.

I figured if they could do it, I could too.

About a year later, after I had returned home and reenrolled in college, I went back to the website to review one of the stories. I searched the page over and over looking for the familiar face, but I couldn't find it. After determining it wasn't a loading glitch on my computer, I started surfing the internet to try to figure out what happened to the inspirational story. When I finally discovered the answer, my heart sunk. The individual, who had previously committed to living a life of celibacy in order to maintain membership in the Church, had fallen in love and married their partner. His story was no longer part of the website.

I took it as a hard loss. It was as if my own plan were threatened as that person's plan changed. I felt angry and disappointed by this person who I had once admired. I judged them and their life choices, thinking they were sinful, weak, lazy, or unfaithful. I imagined they had stopped praying and reading their scriptures. I resented them for following the ways of the world and defaulting to the "easier" path. I thought that if they didn't actually mean what they said about staying single and staying in the Church, they never should have said it at all. I was glad their story was erased.

But I watched this happen over and over and over again. The exemplars of my hope dashed it to pieces. Sometimes it was a feature story on Mormon and Gay, other times it was a popular gay LDS blogger. I watched multiple public mixed-orientation marriages end in divorce, and many high-profile "celibate gays" fall in love. Over the course of a few years I started to wonder why nobody seemed to notice the pattern playing out. We kept prescribing the same solution to "the gay issue," but it rarely yielded the desired results.

As I started paying more attention, I noticed other another troubling social trend: LGBTQ individuals who left the church were dismissed and treated like outcasts. There were a few members of my home ward who had come out as gay, and many times when they were brought up it was salacious and taboo. Conversations in the church hallway were full of hushed tones and tsk tsks.

"Such a shame they would do that to their parents."

"And they came from such a good family."

"Why do they always jump off the deep end?"

People in same-sex relationships were spoken of with fear and judgment. In fact, they weren't really people at all, just dangerous rumors. Those who most needed love, connection, and safety were outcasted by the membership of the Church. Those whose stories and experiences we needed most were the ones whose testimonies, lives, and contributions were considered invalid after they were pushed away. There was a loud, unspoken message in the cancel culture that plagued gay Latter-day Saints.

> **Those who most needed love, connection, and safety were outcasted by the membership of the Church.**

While there has been some degree of improvement among the way LGBTQ members are treated in the Church, that cancel culture still prevails. Standard protocol when an LGBTQ person leaves is to cut them off. I understand why, because people want to protect themselves from any spiritual ailments that might lead them astray. But when we stop associating with people who leave, we never get the full story as to why they weren't able to make it work. We often hold those same assumptions—that they are sinful, weak, lazy, or unfaithful—and never come to understand the real reason why gay people stop coming to Church.

So I want to share why I almost did.

As I tell this next story, I invite you to please try to put yourself in my shoes. Some of what I say will be uncomfortable to read. I admittedly considered filtering my experience or using softer language to make readers more comfortable, but I feel it's really important to share this story how it happened. I want to give you a real, unfiltered look into my past. I ask that you please don't let any discomfort shut you off, but instead use it to gain a greater understanding of what it's like for me to be a gay member of The Church of Jesus Christ of Latter-day Saints. Please make space for this perspective you may have never heard.

* * *

My buddy Austin and I have been friends ever since I can remember. There wasn't a whole lot to do growing up in southwest Missouri, but we were masters at keeping ourselves entertained. We would crash wedding parties, jump in the river, prank our cousins, go on scavenger hunts, and make amateur music videos. Once, we dedicated a whole afternoon to riding one of the cows that periodically wandered too close to his house. With Austin, you didn't have to wait for fun—it was there before you even showed up.

At fourteen years old, after taking a cross-country road trip to Provo for EFY, we both vowed to get into BYU and become roommates. Four years later we got our acceptance emails while at a homecoming dance. I'll never forget sprinting around the school hallways, jumping off benches, and leaping into the air as our dreams became reality. We took the same classes our first semester, and burst onto the scene at the freshman dorms as two small-town Missouri boys trying to make a name for themselves.

Our mission assignments arrived on the same day. Austin was called to Brazil, and I was called to San Bernardino, California. For the next two years our letters flew across the western hemisphere, keeping each other in the loop about crazy mission experiences and everyday miracles. We didn't miss a beat when we got home. We reenrolled in school, found an apartment, and continued our weekly schedule of hiking, party crashing, planning group dates, and drinking absurd amounts of chocolate milk.

Austin met Emily during our senior year of college and was completely smitten. I had been a firsthand witness to all his previous relationships, so I immediately knew Emily was different. When he introduced her to me on their fourth date, he was so nervous that he forgot her name. I wouldn't let him live it down (and probably never will), but she took it in stride with a quick joke and a laugh. She had an unbothered, nonchalant goodness that emanated from her. They were a quirky and natural and fit together, like cake and ice cream.

I spent weeks planning Austin's bachelor party, and it was sure to be a rager. Having all of our buddies back together would have been a party in and of itself, but we pulled out all the stops for Austin. We met up at a ski resort and spent the whole afternoon shredding the slopes. It was a perfect day, with fresh powdery snow and not a cloud in sight. Once the ski lift closed, we headed to a massive rental property that had a hot tub and an indoor pool. We pulled an all-nighter with pizza, drinks, games, and music. We shoved Austin's face in a cake and spent the whole night horsing around and throwing each other in the pool.

As the wedding day arrived, I took it upon myself to be the best best man there ever was, and ran errands all morning to ensure the day was perfect. When the happy couple took bridal pictures, I fluffed Emily's veil, adjusted her train, and held her bouquet between shots. They both looked so happy, and I couldn't have been more excited for them.

A few minutes before the ceremony, we filed into the Provo City Center Temple and lined up at the mouth of a staircase on the first floor. We followed the carpet runner up the stairs and moved into one of the gorgeous sealing rooms. Huge mirrors on adjacent walls hung across from each other, creating an endless tunnel of reflection across the altar that sat in the middle of the room. I looked around at family and friends I had known since childhood and felt so honored to have a front row seat for such a special occasion.

The ceremony was flawless. I'd never been to a live sealing before, and I hung on every word while the couple knelt at the altar. Austin and Emily stared deep into each other's eyes, their faces framed by huge, genuine, toothy smiles. They were glowing—positively beaming with happiness and love.

It was so beautiful; I was so happy for them.

And yet, at the same time, I was completely devastated.

I had done some dating during the year before Austin's wedding. I was extremely cautious and prayerful about the decision, and after a few months of living in New York City, I felt like it was time. I met with the my bishop first, who told me his ward would be a safe place to figure out who I am and what I wanted. He counseled me to stand in holy places and keep the law of chastity, but affirmed that God trusted me and I should trust myself as well.

I dated like a returned missionary. I was prayerful about each man I spent time with and kept all the values and standards I had been instilled with since childhood. Some of the experiences I had were incredibly difficult. I met people who mocked my beliefs or pressured me to do things I wasn't comfortable with. I never knew how naive I had been until I came into the gay dating scene. I was a twenty-four-year-old man with the dating experience of a freshman in high school. I had to learn a lot of lessons I had missed out on during adolescence. I experienced insecurity and heartbreak like I never had before.

In other ways, it was so incredibly beautiful. Dating men was very different from dating women. I learned what it meant to feel butterflies. I got excited to receive text messages or plan cute activities. Love songs started to make sense to me. I understood why people went crazy when they had a crush, and the beautiful distraction of thinking about somebody you like all day long. For the first time ever, I started to feel more like a human and less like a robot. I learned how to communicate more effectively and how to open up vulnerable parts of myself I thought would be closed forever. I met some really incredible guys who respected me and supported my values, and had so much fun discovering new parts of the city with them.

As exciting, new, difficult, and convoluted as dating was, the most difficult feeling was the weight attached to it all. I knew if I found someone I loved, keeping them would eventually come at the cost of fully participating in my religion. As wonderful, kind, attractive, respectful, and compatible as some of the guys I was dating were, I could never fully commit and let them in because I knew what would happen. Furthering a relationship was synonymous with cutting off Church membership. If Austin pursued love, it would lead to marriage and family. If I did the same thing, it would lead to a Church disciplinary council. I could be as pure, faithful, and worthy as anyone alive up until the day I got married. Then, I could immediately lose every right and privilege that came with Church membership. I would no longer be allowed in the temple. I would no longer be offered the sacrament. I could no longer bear my testimony or share my experiences.

Love was exile.

As I sat in Austin and Emily's sealing, listening to the ordinance was a dagger to my heart. I couldn't help but think how badly I wanted the opportunity they had. I imagined myself with a husband at the altar, promising my soul to him. I desperately wished I could dedicate eternity to the one I loved and have our relationship honored by the Church. It was crushing to watch Austin and Emily get the thing I wanted most, knowing it would never be offered to me. As hard as I tried to focus on Austin and Emily—to overwhelm myself with joy for their relationship and their happiness—my lacerating pain would not subside.

Love was exile.

And here it was—a split. Austin and I had spent our entire lives together, hitting every major milestone within days of each other. But in this single moment, our parallel lives became perpendicular. He would move on to family, fatherhood, priesthood callings, progeny, and I would move on to nothing. As similar as we were, this one, overarching difference would forever affect the trajectory of our lives. He would be a husband and a leader, and I would be an outcast.

I walked out of the temple a stone.

I had best man duties for the rest of the day, so I shoved everything I felt to the back corner of my mind and went on autopilot. I chatted with family members, arranged people for group pictures, and pinned boutonnieres on groomsmen. I went to the wedding luncheon, moved tables, and helped with last-minute decorations at the venue. I emceed the reception, gave a toast, decorated the car, and danced the night away. I went to sleep exhausted, forcing my emotions deep within me until I could deal with them on my own. Then in the morning I flew back to New York.

By the time I arrived at my apartment in Manhattan, I was obliterated. I wanted anything to escape the madness I felt. Anger flooded my veins. The pain and ostracization I had buried since childhood bellowed inside me and sprung out like a hot, venomous geyser. I was wholly defeated. I felt like it didn't matter how good I was or how much faith I had; my battle had been decided the day I was born. I was dedicated to a Church that had no place for me.

I tried going for a walk to calm my frazzled state of mind, but I ended up trudging through the cold, empty city streets like a zombie. My pain manifested in flooding waves of anger until I vomited in a bush. I was a dramatic, crazed, shell of a man, haunting the edges of Central Park with no life and no direction.

* * *

This story is difficult for me to tell, and perhaps even harder for others to hear. I struggled to know whether I should share it at all. I often feel like my feelings and my testimony are only considered valid if I'm talking about how dedicated I am to the gospel. People love when I share the beautiful, empowering parts of my faith and Church membership, but tend to back away or take offense if I even mention that being a member of this Church is hard. It seems the minute I say something uncomfortable, people stop listening. It's easy to love the guy on the cover of *LDS Living* who talks about how much he loves the Church, but it's harder to listen when he says things are not working.

But they're not.

I've watched many members become incredibly judgmental toward LGBTQ people who leave the Church. Those who leave are often criticized, especially if they renounce their beliefs, make radical life changes, or become vindictive and bitter toward the Church. But what you see is the poison-dipped tip of the iceberg—weaponized anger to mask the pain. If you look beyond that anger and uncover the primary emotion, you will find heartache. You will find people who tried everything they could to stay in the Church and still couldn't find a place for themselves.

You will see countless years of taxing misconceptions, shifting policies, and frequent invalidations. You will find harrowing stories of loneliness and misunderstanding, and a lifelong struggle to feel God's love.

You will find me, walking alone through the empty streets of New York City, contemplating taking my own life.

Being a gay member of The Church of Jesus Christ of Latter-day Saints is agonizing. My identity, combined with the faith I have, is grief in isolation. There is nothing on any Church website that could have ever prepared me for that low. There is no advice, no conviction, and no mortal reassurance that could solve my hurt. With all my heart I love my faith. Yet, at the same time, I understand why many LGBTQ people leave. For me, it seemed like the only way to be free from my anguish. It was a tragic solution of compromise—a way to calm my inner turmoil by removing the source of my pain.

> **With all my heart I love my faith. Yet, at the same time, I understand why many LGBTQ people leave.**

In Christ's parable of the good Samaritan, He tells of a man on the road to Jericho who fell among thieves and was stripped, beaten, and left half dead. A priest came by, seeing him lying in agony, but he walked around to pass on the other side. Later, a Levite arrived and did the same thing. When a Samaritan saw the scene, however, he stopped. Even though it came at great personal cost, the Samaritan lowered himself to bandage the bloody wounds and help the man in his pain. He then took the injured man to an inn, using his own donkey as transportation.

Once there, he arranged for medical care and promised to return and pay for any cost incurred.

All over the Church there are LGBTQ individuals laying stripped, beaten, and left half dead. There are priests who notice, but because they are so committed to their beliefs, they don't stop to help. Instead, they judge the wounded for their situation, assuming temptation and poor choices led them there. They say something like, "If he could just marry a woman, he wouldn't have these problems. He could stay on the covenant path and be exalted." And they walk on by.

Then there are Levites. They, too, notice the wounded souls but divert their paths to avoid involvement. They look over in pity but won't deal with the social implications of being associated with a gay person. In passing, they say things like, "If he would just stay single and committed to his covenants, this wouldn't be an issue." When the wounded man cries out, they think, "Why does he have to be so loud about it?" And they continue to walk on by.

There is no easy solution to the pain I described the night after Austin's wedding. Judgment, avoidance, or suggestions of marriage or celibacy do nothing to alleviate that anguish. They might solve a traveler's own personal dissonance, but in the end these quick-fix "solutions" are just ways divert their own paths and walk on by. People like me, in the Church, will still be vulnerable, downtrodden, and lying half-dead.

Where are the Samaritans?

The situation in the Savior's parable was dire. The wounded man had no other options. He was bleeding out in a barren desert, far from food, water, or aid. If the Samaritan hadn't stopped, he surely would have died. The plight of God's gay children is equally dire. LGBTQ members of the Church are dying spiritually because not enough Samaritans are stopping to help. There are too few tending to the number of wounded, and too many who walk on by.

> **LGBTQ members of the Church are dying spiritually because not enough Samaritans are stopping to help.**

Who will champion the care of God's gay children?

Who will climb off their donkey and climb into our pain? Who will use their own bandages to bind our wounds and not recoil if they get bloody. Who will sweat in the desert sun to acquire the empathy only earned through lifting us, carrying us, and delivering us to the inn?

If the gay Saint in your congregation hasn't already, they will eventually walk their own "empty street of New York." As they encounter this unresolved agony, do you whisper in the hallways and offer useless solutions? Do you diminish their pain, and get annoyed when they cry out? Do you label their actions "jumping off the deep end," and forget to consider what pushed them there? Do you scorn them for dating, and fade from their lives? Do you judge them when they die—never to step foot in a chapel again?

Do you pass them by on the road to Jericho?

It's difficult to accept that something so meaningful and beautiful to one person can be so painful and challenging for another. Questions surrounding sexual orientation, faith, and Church membership are so awkward, so uncomfortable, and so confusing you might not want to think about them. And to be honest, maybe you don't have to. Perhaps you can say something like, "We don't know everything, but it will all work out in the end" and move on with your life.

But I can't. I don't have that luxury. These questions *are* my life. They permeate my existence.

Guidance won't come on its own. The bedrock of information essential to supporting LGBTQ Latter-day Saints is found only by crawling into their pain. Intimate proximity to the stories, hearts, and heartbreak of gay Latter-day saints will lead to the right questions, the right prayers, and the right answers. As President Russell M. Nelson taught, "Good inspiration is based upon good information"[25] If each member of the Church spent one sleepless night thinking about this for every hundred nights I have, perhaps it would lead them stop next time they saw a wounded traveler on their way to Jericho.

Pity and sorrow are not enough. As a gay member of the Church, I don't want to be cried for, I want to be helped. Feeling sorry for the wounded won't bind their wounds. Empathy without action is empty. As covenant people saved for the latter-days, we *have* to do better. We need to seek inspiration and help all God's children feel love and belonging within the gospel of Christ.

Empathy without action is empty.

We can't keep taking the same approach and expecting different results. "[Spinning] our wheels in the memories of yesterday"[26] will only lead to more deaths on the way to Jericho. We need to study, wrestle, and pray with loving hearts and open minds. Instead of giving inexperienced advice, we need to ask

---

25 Russell M. Nelson, "Revelation for the Church, Revelation for Our Lives," *Ensign,* May 2018.

26 Russell M. Nelson, "A New Normal," *Ensign,* November 2020.

genuine, honest questions. We have to stop judging people who leave and start asking ourselves why. After years in this space, I've seen that many LGBTQ people don't leave the Church, but rather the people of the Church leave them. We must no longer be content with our incomplete Zion—apathetic to the glaring absence of God's LGBTQ children.

* * *

I am no longer the man who was alone on those dark city streets. I was plucked from that pain because someone made space for me. Just before Austin's wedding, I had submitted an opinion article to the *Deseret News*. It was my double coming-out as gay and as Cosmo the Cougar. I felt prompted to write the article in efforts to break down the us vs. them mentality that characterizes the issue. I wanted to help show members of the Church the importance of showing visible love and support to LGBTQ individuals. I doubted it would ever circulate, but I went ahead and submitted it anyway.

As I was weighing whether or not to leave the Church after the wedding, my article was published. I had no idea how much reach it would garner. Within just a few hours it became one of the top news stories in the nation. The positive response sparked the last bit of hope inside of me and pulled me out of despair. As if doused with a bucket of ice water, my spirit awoke with an intense desire to speak for the voiceless. I found purpose in sharing my journey with others and building Zion from within. God parted my Red Sea, provided me with daily bread and a pillar of light. He gave me the strength I needed to move through the wilderness and toward a more promised land.

But this came with a heavy burden. People now look to me to give them advice on how to reconcile faith and orientation. I have done countless news interviews, firesides, and podcasts, and have even written books. I have freely shared the most sacred, scary parts of my life. As miraculous, meaningful, and transformative as it can be, I feel immense pressure at this public convergence of faith and sexuality. I am idolized, idealized, and admired while simultaneously scrutinized, judged, and hated. My story has been used as a healing balm, but also as a weapon. People make blanket assumptions about who I am, what I believe, and where my life is headed. I am told I am too loud, not loud enough, too edgy, too soft. I am accused of being brainwashed, toxic, evil, deceived—everything under the sun. The immense pressure I go through every day is like walking a tightrope through a swarm of mosquitos.

Now that I am in their position, it's hard to believe I once judged the other "poster children" for leaving the Church. In so many ways, their story is my story. The pain and pressure I feel as a gay Latter-day Saint is nearly impossible to bear. Had I undergone the aftermath of Austin's wedding in the public eye, I would have crumbled. I was so wrong to critique those pioneer LGBTQ Saints for falling in love or "falling away." I had no idea what they were up against or what they had been required to give. I never got to know their whole story. I should have offered them grace, but instead, whenever their lives made me uncomfortable, I subjected them to erasure, as did the membership of the Church. I've seen this cycle repeat over and over again. Now, I'm terrified that if I ever choose something that makes people uncomfortable, my story will be erased, too.

By dismissing LGBTQ Saints and erasing their stories, we not only lose them, but we also lose out on crucial knowledge that will help us make Zion stronger. We can't afford to have their experiences pushed outside our boundaries. Understanding the difficult and uncomfortable parts of their stories won't tarnish the membership but will help us keep this spiritually destructive cycle from repeating. When gay Saints are left to die in the desert, we can't carry on like nothing is wrong. We have to stop on the way to Jericho.

The Samaritan's role was not to solve everything; it was to approach the fallen traveler, dress his wounds, and carry him to the inn. The Samaritan knew the inn was safe, and his efforts ensured the traveler would be well cared for. So it may be with us. As it stands now, I don't think there's a perfect solution for gay members of the Church. There's no way for anyone to fix the situation altogether. Thus, our role is to see fallen travelers, meet them in their pain, and ensure our inn is a safe place to land—a place where the wounded will be embraced by Christlike love.

I believe God has answers and further light and knowledge for His children. I know "He will yet reveal many great and important things pertaining to the Kingdom of God,"[27] for as prophets have proclaimed, "The promised Restoration goes forward through continuing revelation. The earth will never again be the same, as God will 'gather together in one all things in Christ' (Ephesians 1:10)."[28] The healing God's LGBTQ children need will ultimately come through Christ alone, and I anticipate His solution will be much grander than anything I could ever imagine. When that time comes,

---

27 Articles of Faith 1:9.

28 "The Restoration of the Fulness of the Gospel of Jesus Christ: A Bicentennial Proclamation to the World," *Ensign*, May 2020.

LGBTQ travelers will be able to make it to Jericho without falling among thieves.

But in the meantime, we need Samaritans.

12.

VISITORS WELCOME

D URING THE SUMMER of 2019, after coming out publicly in an op-ed piece for the *Deseret News*, I was selected to be part of AT&T's Turn Up the Love: Young Heroes campaign. The project consisted of a six-part docuseries highlighting stories of different LGBTQ individuals who were making positive changes in their respective communities. I was honored to be chosen for the project and looked forward to it with immense anticipation.

The first day of filming took place at the Salt Lake City Pride parade. The plan was to collect B-footage of me leading the AT&T float, then move to a different location to film an interview portion later in the afternoon. I woke up early with excitement, making sure to iron my outfit, fix my hair, and put on what I now recognize as way too much cologne. I arrived at the provided address—a historic hotel in the downtown area—right on time and walked into the lobby to meet the film crew.

To my surprise, there was a whole production team, complete with cameras, lighting equipment, sound booms, and microphones. After meeting with the director, I was sent to a hair and makeup team to ensure my appearance was flawless before the parade began. We spent a few minutes going over the plan and brainstorming footage ideas, then lined up with the rest of the floats in the parade. While waiting, I was introduced to various social media influencers, celebrity guests, and advocacy leaders in the LGBTQ community.

For the next hour I felt like a celebrity myself. Surrounded by the film crew, I enthusiastically led one of the largest floats in the parade. The streets were flanked by thousands of people dressed in bright colors, cheering us on as we marched. I started showboating, doing series of back handsprings and flips down the streets as the parade slowly moved through the city. Every now and then the makeup artist would run over to touch up my face, brushing translucent powder onto my forehead to make sure I never looked sweaty or shiny on camera.

Growing up, I had always viewed Pride parades at *best* as unnecessary celebrations of something that didn't matter much. Before coming out, it seemed strange that people wanted to flaunt their sexuality in such an ostentatious way. I'd heard other people refer to them as celebrations of sin, using phrases like "the dissolution of the traditional family" and "a dangerous sign of the times." Marching in a parade surrounded by rainbow flags wasn't something I'd ever imagined myself doing.

But now that I was here, I couldn't help but feel overwhelmed by the emotions that overtook me. I thought of myself as a teenager, bathed in self-hatred and distress due to my orientation. There were years I would have rather been dead than gay. I viewed my orientation as a disgusting, carnal wedge that would keep me from everything I loved. The thought of anyone knowing this vulnerable, terrifying part of me filled me with dread, and I constantly attacked myself in efforts to change.

I never dreamed I could confidently march in public, letting everyone know my once most guarded secret. I had overcome the embarrassment, contempt, and suicidality of my past. I felt brighter and more hopeful than ever. I was reminded of Isaiah 54:4: "For thou shalt not be ashamed: neither be thou confounded; for thou shalt not be put to shame: for thou shalt forget the shame of thy youth." I had family and friends who loved me, relationships that had been strengthened, and peace of mind that allowed me to look to the future with more hope.

It was especially meaningful to be in Salt Lake for this moment. In the place where I most feared how my community might view me, I wasn't heckled or mocked for being me. On the contrary, I was celebrated. Thousands of strangers lined the streets to offer me, and everyone else like me, love, encouragement, and support.

I realized why the event was called Pride: because I felt the exact opposite of shame.

I continued marching down the street and entertaining the crowd with my flips. I took selfies with strangers and reveled in every moment. I felt like my life was a dream, with nothing out of place.

That is, until I saw a church steeple peek out from a gap in the city skyline.

I remembered it was Sunday, the day I held sacred for worshipping my Creator. Suddenly, I felt completely torn. I wanted the healing and inspiration that came from marching in the Pride parade—my soul needed it. But it also needed the calm, peaceful assurance that could only come from honoring the

Sabbath and renewing my baptismal covenants. I pulled my attention away from the parade, grabbed my phone, and checked the meetinghouse's Sunday service schedule. The ward started at 11:00 a.m.—it was 10:53.

I expressed silent frustration at whoever planned the Pride events. Did they have to schedule this on Sunday morning? Couldn't it have fit somewhere else? Weren't there other people here who wanted to go to church this week? But I kind of already knew the answer to that. That's part of the reason everyone found me so fascinating—the former BYU mascot who came out as gay but still went to church—the man who refused to pick a side. I knew, at least among the crowd this morning, I was probably an anomaly.

I tried to push thoughts of going to church to the far corner of my mind. I couldn't just dip out on the parade. There was an entire production crew who had flown out from Los Angeles just to film me. I was booked for the entire day. I couldn't just disappear because I wanted to go to church. Besides, sacrament meeting happened every week. Being featured in a docuseries was a once-in-a-lifetime opportunity. There was really only one right decision.

But as I was walking, I no longer felt happy. It seemed hypocritical to celebrate embracing my full, authentic self in a Pride parade when it required putting my religious identity on the back burner. I was gay—yes—but I was also a disciple of Jesus Christ. Why did the two have to be at such odds with each other? Why did society make it so hard to choose both?

Eventually, I couldn't take it anymore. I walked over to the film director and explained there was something important I needed to do. I asked if it would be okay if I took an hour off from filming, promising to return as soon as possible. He checked his schedule and said he could probably push a few things around. He said if I could get back right at noon my absence wouldn't be too much of an issue.

Why did society make it so hard to choose both?

With a rush of relief, I slipped out of the parade procession and made my way through the crowd. Once free, I all but ran to the chapel. I arrived at an older, red brick building with stained-glass accent windows. A carved stone inlay was displayed at the front with words that read, "The Church of Jesus Christ of Latter-day Saints. Visitors Welcome." I checked the time, satisfied to see I was only a few minutes late. I rushed up to the glass doors, eager to go in.

But when I caught a glimpse of myself in the reflection, I paused. I had been so caught up with getting there before the meeting started, I hadn't taken my wardrobe into consideration. I was wearing khaki shorts and a black T-shirt—far from standard Sunday attire. To make things worse, I had on white socks with colored accents, tennis shoes, and a rainbow-striped belt. I wasn't used to going to church in anything but a white shirt and tie. My outfit was perfect for filming a Pride campaign, but at an LDS Church service it would stick out wildly.

I knew if I walked into the ward building, everyone there would immediately know I was gay. It would be obvious I was coming directly from Pride. I recalled the sign I on the building: "Visitors Welcome." Did that include gay visitors? What if they weren't wearing the right outfit? Was I even a visitor at all? I was a Melchizedek Priesthood holder with a temple recommend. Why did I feel like such an exile?

Is this worth it?

I was met with a familiar feeling of never having a place. I longed for a world where two of the most important aspects of my identity weren't always at such odds. There was a clear social place for gay people, and a clear social place for members of the Church of Jesus Christ, but for me, whose life sat on the intersection of both, little was ever clear. Going to church often meant feeling awkward, judged, and alone. But I still wanted to be there, and I knew choosing between my faith and my orientation would never make me happy. I needed to choose both.

> **I longed for a world where two of the most important aspects of my identity weren't always at such odds.**

From the foyer I heard the bishop welcoming the congregation. I scanned the room until I spotted an open seat on the far side of the church. With a deep breath, I took courage and began making my way across the chapel, welcomed by the familiar sounds and smell of sacrament meeting.

Just then, the bishop's voice bellowed through the sound system. "Thank you, brothers and sisters, for being here today." He said tersely, "It warms my soul to see you all in the Lord's house, safe from the evils overtaking the streets downtown."

What?

My jaw dropped.

Did he just say what I thought he said? Did he mean . . . ?

My nerves went numb.

He was talking about the Pride parade—the place where I had just come from.

I became acutely aware that I was a tall, casually dressed outsider in a rainbow belt, moving in plain view of the entire room. Whatever courage I'd had walking in the doors was shot dead by the bishop's comment. Suddenly, my entire being was focused on trying not to cry. I thought about running out, but somehow that felt even more embarrassing. I moved as quickly as I could toward the open pew, but it didn't matter—there was no way to hide. Whispers swept over the congregation. Members shuffled in their seats, craning their necks to catch a glimpse of me: the "evil" that had traipsed in from the streets downtown.

I wished I would have stayed at the Pride parade. I felt so much safer there.

I sank into the pew as the opening hymn was announced, my heart beating uncontrollably. Most people started redirecting their attention to their hymnals, but the woman nearest to me kept glancing back and forth between the pulpit and my outfit. She looked incredibly uncomfortable. I imagined the thoughts running through her mind . . . "Why is he here? I don't like him sitting so close to my kids."

She leaned toward me.

I braced for impact.

"Hi! I'm Katie," she said with a smile that was somehow both sad and earnest. "Welcome to church.

"Uh . . . thanks," I said, still dazed by my traumatizing entrance.

"I'm so glad you're here. Are you familiar with how the service works?" she asked.

"Yeah. I am. Thank you," I replied.

"Great! Well let me know if you need anything. I really am so happy you're here with us."

Katie turned back around and started rummaging through a giant diaper bag. She pulled out some snacks and toys for her two young children, then grabbed her hymnbook and flipped to number 227, "There is Sunshine in My Soul Today." As she placed the diaper bag back on the floor, I noticed a rainbow pin attached to one of the flaps. It had an inscription on it that said, "You Belong."

* * *

It couldn't have been harder for me to go to church that day. It was logistically difficult, I was wearing the wrong outfit, and I felt ostracized before I ever entered the building. Once there, I got burned by my own people. In the church I belonged to—the one I had sacrificed so much to build throughout my life—I was publicly humiliated. At that point, it was almost as if my conviction didn't matter. I wished I hadn't gone at all.

The only sunshine in my soul during that meeting was Katie. Her gesture didn't take away the bishop's comment, nor did it reverse the gaping stares, but it did make me feel like, to at least one person, I was welcome. Her small effort helped me feel more comfortable to renew my covenants and worship my Savior—the very reason I had worked so hard to attend.

What would my story have looked like without her?

When I consider the quandary of LGBTQ members of the Church of Jesus Christ, it reminds me of a story from the Book of Mormon. As Alma and Amulek were proselyting in the land of Nephi, they came across an underprivileged group of Zoramites who weren't allowed to worship with the rest of their community. They had "labored abundantly to build [synagogues with their] own hands" but they were "esteemed by their brethren as dross" and considered filthy because of how poor they were. Even despite their tremendous efforts to construct the synagogues, "they were not permitted to enter into [them] to worship" (Alma 32:5, 3).

Countless LGBTQ Latter-day Saints dedicate their lives to building the Church. They are blessed with unique abilities, and many pour their whole souls into service, building up God's earthly kingdom. They are missionaries, teachers, and leaders. They lend their talents, their skills, and their voices to beautify and replenish congregations. Unfortunately, after coming out, gay Saints often feel dismissed and rejected. Their contributions are devalued once people know they're gay. They, like the Zoramites, are esteemed as "dross" and no longer feel comfortable in the "synagogues."

My friend Lucas grew up incredibly devoted to the gospel. He came from a devout family, descended from pioneer ancestors. As a youth, he served in various capacities within the Aaronic Priesthood and frequently volunteered to help members of his ward. Lucas loved being a part of the Church and was an "example of the believers, in word, in conversation, in charity, in spirit, in faith, in purity" (1 Timothy 4:12)

After high school, Lucas was admitted to a top-tier university on full scholarship, but he declined the offer to serve a mission. Instead of pursuing his Ivy League dreams, he went to proselyte in the ivy jungles of Brazil. While there, he built up the Church by not only teaching and baptizing but also by playing the piano on Sundays and offering service to the members of the congregation. When Lucas returned from his mission, he served as elders quorum president and ward organist. He organized a stake choir, served in the temple, volunteered as a "mock investigator" at the Missionary Training Center, and was a favorite youth counselor at FSY. Lucas's life was dedicated to serving others and building the Church.

Once Lucas came out as gay, however, people started treating him differently. He was released from his priesthood calling and replaced as stake choir director. Soon after, a friend in the ward sent him a message saying she didn't want her friends to think she "condoned sinful lifestyles" and would probably stop hanging out with him to "avoid the appearance of evil." Later, his bishop told him other ward members had expressed alarm, and that it might be best to limit comments he made during Sunday school. Lucas explained that he still had a desire to serve and would never make any comments contrary to gospel doctrine, but his bishop doubled down. Lucas felt hurt, dismissed, and ignored by his leaders and his peers. His contact with the Church slowly faded until it became obsolete.

"I still have a testimony," Lucas told me. "I pray every night and study the scriptures each morning. I even listen to conference talks sometimes on my commute. . . . But I got to the point where I couldn't go to church anymore. I wanted them, but they didn't want me."

Lucas never had a Katie.

Romans 14:10 reads, "But why dost thou judge thy brother? or why dost thou set at nought thy brother? for we shall all stand before the judgment seat of Christ." Though we are explicitly commanded not to judge, sometimes it seems that counsel goes out the window when it comes to our LGBTQ friends and neighbors. In efforts to "avoid the appearance of evil" or not "condone sin," Church members often judge and distance themselves from members of the LGBTQ community. Even I, as a single member in full fellowship, knew that leaving the Pride parade to renew my covenants would mean subjecting myself to judgment. It's why I paused outside the doors to worry about my outfit, and why I fought back tears as I rushed to my seat.

In that well-meaning bishop's mind, by making his comment, he was defending truth. He was sticking up for the traditional family and making the Church a fortress against influence from the outside world. But his approach marginalized me. They made a son of God feel unwelcome in the Lord's house. By contrast, Katie operated with a more inclusionary view of Zion. To her, the Church wasn't a fortress, but a refuge. With kind words, a smile, and a rainbow pin on her diaper bag, she acted as a Samaritan and carved out a space for me to worship. She brought me closer to Christ.

LGBTQ people don't just belong in our meetinghouses—they are needed. They are creative, generous, valuable souls who can enrich our communities and enhance our worship. Their testimonies are forged in unimaginable ways. Consider the faith required to navigate their eternal unknown! Their unique need for reliance on the Lord mirrors that of Nephi himself, forging through the wilderness in hopes of a promised land. Their belief and commitment to gospel principles is unparalleled. It's the kind of conviction that compelled me to leave a documentary crew to take the sacrament in an intolerant ward, and Lucas to still listen to conference talks on his drive to work.

> **LGBTQ people don't just belong in our meetinghouses—they are needed.**

Members of the Church of Jesus Christ need what LGBTQ individuals have to offer. We need their dynamic leadership. We need their artistic abilities. We need their rare perspectives, creative minds, and invigorating spirits.

God's LGBTQ children are indispensable.

The Book of Mormon describes the beloved, happy state of Zion achieved by the ancient people of God. 4 Nephi 1:15–17 reads, "And it came to pass that there was no contention in the land, because of the love of God which did dwell in the hearts of the people . . . and surely there could not be a happier people among all the people who had been created by the hand of God. There were no . . . Lamanites, nor any manner of -ites; but they were in one, the children of Christ, and heirs to the kingdom of God."

For too long, God's gay children have been -ites. We can no longer afford to treat them as such. We must enlarge our view of Zion and include LGBTQ people in it. As Christ Himself commanded, "Behold, ye shall meet together oft; and ye shall not forbid any man from coming unto you when ye shall meet together, but suffer them that they may come unto you and forbid them not; But ye shall pray for them, and shall not cast them out; and if it so be that they come unto you oft ye shall pray for them unto the Father, in my name" (3 Nephi 18:22–23).

We must enlarge our view of Zion and include LGBTQ people in it.

No one should feel safer at a Pride parade than they do in sacrament meeting. No one's effort to worship should be met with craned necks and capricious stares. God's love is all-encompassing, and we must build our congregations to match.

By expanding the borders of Zion, and being like Katie, we can foster environments that embody the words etched in stone on the side of each meetinghouse:

Visitors Welcome.

13.

THIS IS THE PLACE

I HELD MY LUGGAGE CLOSE as I shuffled my way through
the underground crowds. It was rush hour, and the transfer
platform was muggy and packed to the brim. Strangers scurried
in various directions, following color-coded signs while a band
played a questionable jazz cover of "Welcome to New York."
The noise bounced off the cavern of tiled walls and muddled
with the attendant's robotic voice crackling through the speakers
overhead: "There is an uptown local '1' train to Van Courtlandt
Park approaching the station. Please stand away from the platform edge."

Navigating the Times Sq.-42 St. subway stop was not for
the faint of heart.

As I fought through the mass, I noticed a young man on
the far end of the platform. He looked distressed, frantically
whipping his head back and forth between the overhead signs
and his phone screen. He reminded me of myself on the day
I first moved to the city. In my childlike excitement, I hadn't

paid attention and hopped on the wrong line, ending up lost somewhere in Chinatown. I had to ask three different people how to get back to my apartment.

I made my way over to the lost newcomer.

"Need help?" I asked amiably.

"Um . . . no, I think I . . ."

He reconsidered.

"Yeah. Yeah, I really do."

I figured out where he was headed and pointed him in the right direction, then squeezed into a downtown E-train toward JFK.

I felt extra weight in my backpack, reminding me that my time in the city might be coming to an end. It was stuffed with university info packets and grad school applications. I'd mostly narrowed my options down to big city schools on either coast, figuring it would be easier for me to fit in. But for some reason, I still felt obligated to consider master's programs in Utah, so I had reluctantly bought a ticket and was headed to the airport.

As I rattled along below ground, I studied a large map of the city displayed on the subway car and began feeling nostalgic. I could see the cross streets where I had come out to my dad, and I thought about how much we had both grown since then. I scanned the West Side, my eyes darting to the apartment where a random book club invite had led me to some of my closest friends. They were the ones who really made New York feel like a home. I traced my daily running loop through Central Park, envisioning the reflection of the city on the reservoir and the cherry trees where I'd meet up with my friend Jack.

Memories came in sequential waves: Broadway shows, afternoons at the Met, weeknights at institute, and a ward trip to Coney Island. I recalled the enchantment of my first real date and how my heartbeat had skipped on the way home. I remembered calling a friend to gush about how cute my date was and how he was so much nicer than I'd expected. I smiled at the thought of the miracle stylist on Lexington Avenue who had fixed my hopelessly damaged bleached hair, and how as I told her about my life I felt a little more of my childhood shame slip away.

In so many ways, the city represented freedom—a place where I didn't have to pretend—a place where I could be me.

But the memories weren't all good.

For a Latter-day Saint from small-town Missouri, tackling the "gay adolescence" in New York had been daunting. My naiveté and lack of experience had led to hard lessons, and even a few dangerous situations. With remorse, I reflected on times my innocence had been challenged by people I never should have trusted. I discovered people who wanted parts of me, but not all of me. The map brought flashbacks of the tumult of my first relationship and the ache of my first real breakup. I relived the humiliation of being mocked and ridiculed for my beliefs, and saw the big cathedral next to my apartment where I used to cry when life got overwhelming. My thoughts turned to the lonely edges of Central Park and the aimless path I had roamed that devastating night after my friend Austin's wedding.

In those times of trial, my faith was indispensable and real. I desperately needed peace, the kind that can only come from the Savior. I kept a Book of Mormon in my backpack, devouring it whenever I could. The words felt alive and fed my withered soul. I lived week to week, yearning for the sacrament and for the opportunity to worship at church. I drew hope from the gospel of Jesus Christ, from membership in my ward, and from seeing Jack and Omar in the pew next to me. They helped me feel worship was possible, no matter how my life looked.

The subway car lurched to a stop and I followed the crowd up the elevators to the SkyTrain. As I thought about moving away, I felt a rush of anxiousness. The LGBTQ Church experience is largely dependent on ward members and local leadership, and I was terrified to leave Manhattan. If my next bishop wasn't comfortable with me being gay, my activity and involvement might be compromised. I'd also face uncertainty if my new ward members weren't accepting. Everything could depend on the city, street, and neighborhood where my next apartment happened to be located. It was like playing roulette. If I landed in the wrong spot, staying active in the Church would be a lot more difficult.

It was also unsettling to not know how I'd feel about relationships in a new place. At the time, dating didn't feel right, so I'd broken up with a guy I'd been seeing. It made my religious life easier, but I wasn't sure if it was sustainable. The older I got, the more difficult it was to be single. Every time a friend got married and started a family, I felt increasingly left behind. I'd probably want a companion eventually—someone to love and share my life with. What would I do then? Being single for lack of finding the right person was one thing, but being single after finding them would be torture.

My thoughts began to scatter. In some ways, I was more lost than the guy on the subway platform. I could navigate New York City with ease, but I was at a loss concerning the direction of my future.

I carried my discomfort through campus tours the next day. I felt like Nephi, but not in a good way. I didn't feel strong or faithful or large in stature. I just felt like I was homeless, wandering the wilderness in search of a promised land. My bow was broken, my Liahona was lost, the company was murmuring, and

I had no idea how to build a boat. To be honest, I wasn't even sure if a promised land existed. Maybe being gay just meant a life in the wilderness, with no place to rest or call home.

I was at a loss concerning the direction of my future.

Later that night, I found even more reason to murmur. I met up with my friend Mark and his husband for dinner, and they told a story that broke me. They had been married for about a year and planned to stay active in their ward. For a while it was working. They sat in the third pew every Sunday, and Mark's husband was even called as ward pianist. For a few months they lived their dream life, full of love for each other and involvement in church.

But that happiness didn't last long. When their local leadership changed, so did their membership status. They were called in for a disciplinary council and admonished to get divorced.

"How could we do that?" Mark asked in disbelief. "How could we break apart our family?"

They chose to stay together, and in a matter of weeks, they were excommunicated—their priesthood stripped and their baptisms revoked. I held it together through dinner, listening to my friends and empathizing with their story, but later that night I completely lost it. I called my sister and yelled my frustrations until I broke into sobs.

The next morning I was still a wreck. I tried working remotely but couldn't find a lick of focus. It was the first time the Church policy had really hit me. I was beside myself, bewildered by the realization that if my friends had stopped attending church, their baptisms would have still been intact. It seemed cruel that the only gay couples subject to Church discipline were the ones who kept showing up on Sundays—a disturbing "reward" for worship.

My thoughts kept spiraling. Was I lying to myself? Did anyone actually want me at church? I thought about Jack and Omar, sitting next to me during sacrament meeting just a few days prior. Would this be their fate? Every negative emotion I'd ever had flooded back to me. I was mad at Church leaders. I was mad at Church culture. I was mad at everything. I was a child with no life preserver, helpless and suffocating. Where was God in all of this? I wanted to rush back to New York—back to safety—but my return flight wasn't for two more days.

I was stuck.

By the time afternoon came, I shut my laptop and went driving to clear my head. I started up Provo Canyon, snaking beneath the shadows of the mountains. I turned back and made my way to Utah Lake, then went north past the point of the mountain and over to Cottonwood Canyon. The drive helped calm my mind.

Eventually, I ended up in Salt lake City, roaming Church history sights and hoping for a sign. I started at Temple Square, touring the visitors' centers and walking the well-known grounds. I circled the area two times, moving through the Conference Center, around the Tabernacle, and to the Assembly Hall. I couldn't help but think about the early Saints who had dedicated their lives to constructing these buildings, and how hard they had worked to find a place where they were free to worship.

Goldenrods and Utah daisies filled the flower beds, and birds chirped in the trees as I meandered around to the Beehive House. From there, I walked past the terraced fountains to the large, oblong reflective pool in front of the temple. I stood there for a while, studying the mirror image of its neo-Gothic granite facade—the image of my heritage—rippling in the water. A couple crossed by in the reflection, newly married and surrounded by loved ones. Their family cheered as they kissed in front of the temple.

It all felt like a mirage.

I walked back to my car.

I made my way east, driving through the old, established neighborhoods toward the mountain until I ended up at This Is the Place Heritage Park. I walked around, exploring the historic buildings, still thinking about the pioneers who built them. I knew their story well. After years of instability, turmoil, and persecution, they finally made it to Zion, a place to rest and call home. How joyful it must have been to crest the mountain and look out at the Salt Lake Valley. I imagined their exuberant exclamations echoing through the wagon trail—"This is the place!"

Looking over the community they built, I wished I felt the same sense of refuge.

I stayed there until nightfall, watching the sun cast an orange glow onto the mountains as it sunk into the western sky. When I made my way back, the interstate was dark, and I was one of few drivers on the road. My headlights illuminated the lane markers, which appeared in flashing stripes as I sped along. I was fixated on the pioneers. I'd made the drive from my home state of Missouri to Salt Lake dozens of times. The route hugged the original Mormon Trail, moving through prairies, planes, mountains, rivers, and hills. Part of me wished I'd had my ancestors' lot in life. I might have been able to handle the physical challenge of being a trail pioneer. I could hunt, start fires, and push a handcart. But the emotional toll of being a gay pioneer was crushing me. I wasn't sure I could make it much further, and I didn't know if there'd ever be a place for me to settle.

I kept driving, dodging construction signs and orange cones. I said the thousandth silent prayer of the day, asking God to give me some sort of direction. My mind buzzed with never-ending thoughts and fears. Everything seemed so unfair.

I switched on the stereo to catch a break from the madness. An old CD of the Tabernacle Choir at Temple Square rose through the speakers.

Come, come, ye Saints, no toil nor labor fear;
But with joy wend your way.

I reached my hand out to switch the music, but something made me pause.

Though hard to you this journey may appear,
Grace shall be as your day.

I felt the Spirit fill the car. The song wasn't playing by chance.

'Tis better far for us to strive
Our useless cares from us to drive;
Do this, and joy your hearts will swell—

As I listened, the words of William Clayton's pioneer anthem transformed into an allegory for my journey as a gay Latter-day Saint. I realized I could give up. God gave me agency, and I could leave the Church anytime I wanted. I could stop trying and eliminate the conflict that swarmed me. But though I knew the journey would surely be difficult, I also knew that for me, it was better to strive. If I wanted to find true joy, I'd have to stick it out and keep wending my way through the wilderness. While there, I would find grace day by day, leading me closer to the journey's end.

Why should we mourn or think our lot is hard?
'Tis not so; all is right.

Why should we think to earn a great reward
If we now shun the fight?

I had so many legitimate reasons to murmur. Because I was gay, there were countless ways I was misunderstood, dismissed, and discriminated against. But maybe, in all of the mess, God had a bigger plan. Maybe I was right where I was supposed to be, developing Christlike characteristics and teaching others how to love. I'd always had faith in a God of miracles—I believed deliverance would eventually come for His LGBTQ children. But maybe in the meantime there were miracles already around me. And, if I truly wanted God to part my Red Sea, how could I expect such a reward if I stopped fighting to keep my faith? Like the pioneers, I would have to carry on.

Maybe, in all of the mess, God had a bigger plan.

Gird up your loins; fresh courage take.
Our God will never us forsake;
And soon we'll have this tale to tell—
All is well! All is well!

I had the profound feeling there *was* a "promised land" for people like me. I didn't know what it would look like, or how it would unfold, but God did. It was time to retrench—to put my faith in Christ like I never had before. Through wilderness, desert, prairies, or snow, I had to be confident God would not forsake me. Tears welled in my eyes as I realized how involved He already was. He was answering every prayer I had offered throughout the day through the words of this hymn.

We'll find the place which God for us prepared,
Far away in the West,

Where none shall come to hurt or make afraid;
There the Saints will be blessed.

The phrase I'd pondered earlier that afternoon came back to me: "This is the place." It almost seemed crazy, but I knew what I needed to do. God had prepared a place for me, here, and I had to move back. I wasn't nervous—I knew it would be different this time. I'd have friends, family, and the support I needed. I'd be safe from the vulnerable situations associated with my gay adolescence and protected by my community. As the choir sang the last line, it took on a double meaning. Not only would I be blessed as a Saint, but my presence would bless others.

We'll make the air with music ring,
Shout praises to our God and King;

That part was already happening. The music was pouring through the speakers, and my heart was bursting with love for my Heavenly Father.

Above the rest these words we'll tell—
All is well! All is well!

When I got back later that night, I rushed to my computer. I looked up prerequisite courses for mental health–related master's programs in Utah and signed up for all of them. I withdrew my applications to every school outside of the state and canceled my return flight to New York City. If God had prepared a place for me here, that's where I would stay. I could figure out logistics later.

Part of me worried I was being rash, but it wasn't long before I found the direction I had been seeking. I started writing, compiling my experiences into a book dedicated to my fourteen-year-old self. The process proved incredibly healing and helped me solidify who I am and what I believe about my identity. It allowed me to give back and feel like I was making the difference only I could make.

As my book moved through the publication process, my friend Ben asked if I would help him start a podcast. We began cohosting a weekly show called *Questions from the Closet*, taking questions from struggling LGBTQ Saints and discussing them with faith-filled guests. Interviewing them not only provided a beneficial and previously nonexistent resource to the community but also gave me more insight and tools for my own path. The days I felt most congruent with my orientation and my faith were the days we recorded for the podcast.

I continued doing my best to build Zion, speaking at firesides and strengthening those in the margins. As I dedicated my life to working in this neglected part of the Lord's vineyard, my circle of love began to increase. I met people from all walks of life, in all corners of the wilderness. The "field [was] white, already to harvest" (D&C 4:4), and I found meaning as I lost myself in the service of others.

Not long after, I was admitted into BYU's master of social work program. The education, advocacy tips, and clinical therapy training I received made me a better minister. I felt passionate about the curriculum and found joy as a student-athlete. During my final year, I was hired as a therapy intern on campus and got to hone my skills with other LGBTQ students at the university. Every day after cheer practice as I walked to my office, I heard familiar notes chime from the bell tower—"Come, Come Ye Saints."

I was still subject to the conflict and instability of being a gay Latter-day Saint. In many cases, it was even augmented by my emergence as a public figure. I was confronted with misunderstanding, hostility, hate, and judgment. But as God had promised, I found a protective community. My younger siblings both returned from missions and moved in with me, and friends both new and old buoyed me up. In time, I met another extraordinary gay man named Ryan, who taught me how to speak my truth and withstand criticism. He healed parts of my heart I didn't know were broken, and helped me grow in patience and love. Even my local Church leaders seemed to be directly called for my sake. When I was attacked on social media, degraded in public, or just needed someone to rant to, I had a core group of people who defended and stood by me.

It was no parade. I got confused. I got worn out. I made mistakes and got caught at the end of my rope. But through every twist, turn, and tumble, the Lord was there for me. He was patient, loving, consistent, and sure, providing a shadow by day and a pillar by night. Through repentance, courage, and faith in His matchless power, I found light and guidance. As I'd felt so surely that night driving home in my car, God truly did prepare a place for me.

Looking back on that empty interstate, enveloped by the sound and spirit of "Come, Come, Ye Saints," there was one final verse that changed me forever. It struck me like no composition ever had before, stirring my heart and awakening my soul.

And should we die before our journey's through,
Happy day! All is well!
We then are free from toil and sorrow, too;
With the just we shall dwell!

I realized that if I, like so many gay Saints before me, gave my best effort and never made it to the "promised land," I would be okay. God would know my efforts and see the faith that had brought me as far as it did. I'd be free from the pain and exertion required to practice my faith and still be able to find happiness. No matter how my life panned out, I was a child of God, and nothing could ever take that away. Christ loved me enough to atone for my sins, and through His grace, I would inherit a kingdom of glory in the next life. My heart was pierced by the very thought of His selfless love.

But if our lives are spared again
To see the Saints their rest obtain,
Oh, how we'll make this chorus swell—
All is well! All is well!

As I heard these words, tears streamed down my face. I'd seen so many of my LGBTQ friends die, both physically and spiritually. I'd watched them wear down beneath the social pressures placed upon them. I'd seen them lose family, lose testimonies, and lose themselves as they drowned in their toil and sorrow. Like chaff, they'd been cast away from Zion. Until that moment, dying in the wilderness had seemed inevitable. It was all I'd ever witnessed.

But God was bigger than the wilderness.

God was bigger than the wilderness.

I imagined a world where His LGBTQ children could find rest with the Saints—free from all pain, shame, isolation, and confusion. I imagined them integrated in Zion, each soul raising their voice in unified song. How grand that chorus would be! Comprised of all God's children, regardless of who they were or how they loved. I imagined myself and other gay individuals falling to our knees in worship, praising our Creator, and reverberating with the same joy and deliverance as the pioneer Saints who entered the Salt Lake Valley so many years ago.

"This is the place."

The vision sent a channel of light that broke through the storm in my heart. I knew it was a long shot, but there, alone in my car, on the middle of Interstate 15, I made a firm resolve to try and get there. If I had to build a boat, cross the plains, or ford a river, I would keep pushing onward. Even if everyone thought I was crazy, I would work tirelessly to create the world I wanted to live in and hold steadfast to my faith in Christ. I would fight like a lion to forge a new path and endeavor to find rest in the promised land.

So I carry on.

I come from a heritage of fighters—faithful believers who crossed seas, pushed handcarts, and settled untamed lands. Their blood flows through my veins, and their faith lives determined in my heart. Being a gay member of The Church of Jesus Christ of Latter-day Saints takes grit, and I have grit. I've held to the iron rod, even when it's left me dangling ten feet in the air. I've worked every day of my life to push through my doubt and keep traveling in this wilderness.

But I have not traveled alone. Each time I have almost died before my journey is through, someone has been there to spare my life and help me obtain rest with the Saints.

When I have slipped through holes in the fence, my friends and family have bushwhacked through the unknown to find me. When I have been labeled a sinner, Saints have communed with me and invited me to their table. When I was scared to share the deepest part of me, an unkempt waitress and a convenience store worker with green hair taught me how to be myself. When I had childhood regrets and wanted to make up for them, a supportive cheer coach put me front and center.

When I was exhausted by the way my voice fell on deaf ears, my brother promised to advocate for me. When I was scared of myself, and for the future of my relationships, a backwoods cake decorator showcased her love. When I was angry at leadership, and disheartened by the Saints, a school administrator bore my burden. When I felt like an outcast and wanted to withdraw, there was a gay man serving in the temple. When I wanted to date, my bishop didn't shun me, but honored my agency and encouraged me to stand in holy places.

At pivotal points in my life, people have asked, "Lord, is it I?" They have actively worked to overcome bias and become vessels for my healing. They have provided crucial support through each stage of coming out and helped me achieve more harmony and synthesis at the complicated intersection of my faith. In my darkest moments, when my soul was tired and my faith all but destroyed, there have been Samaritans who have diverted their path, bound up my wounds, and carried me to the inn.

Sometimes it seems like there's a boundary—an exclusionary line—that keeps LGBTQ individuals out of the Church. But somehow, there has always been someone there to stretch that line just far enough to create room for me. Against all odds, they have annexed me into Zion and carved out a place for me to belong.

It's time we do the same for all of God's children.

For our chorus to swell, we need everyone with us, regardless of orientation or identity. We need each unique voice to sing out, with a clear and honored place in the choir. Only then can those illustrious words ring true:

All is well! All is well!

For our chorus to swell, we need everyone with us.

To the LGBTQ or same-sex attracted reader, I testify of your divinity. You were created intentionally, sent to earth by sacred design. The light and perspective you carry is invaluable—an indispensable gift to the world. You are loved, you are needed, and you are not alone. I pray you'll find strength and rejuvenation as you travel this wilderness, and allies who shoulder your load. I have faith and hope in a God of deliverance. Someday we'll crest the mountains to discover our refuge. Someday we'll have a place to belong, where we can dwell and worship with the Saints.

To the reader seeking to learn, I wholeheartedly thank you for engaging in the wrestle. I'm humbled by your willingness to challenge discomfort and your desire to enlarge your capacity to love. Within the doctrine of the restored Church of Jesus Christ, there truly is more room that can be made for God's LGBTQ children. Please take stewardship over this overlooked part of the Lord's vineyard. Surely it will not be easy. It will take consistent effort, regular introspection, and Christlike sacrifice to root out old practices that keep Zion's borders closed. But even through this difficulty, I pray that you, as covenant members of the Christ's Church, will lead out in this effort. You have the power to cultivate belonging for LGBTQ people both inside and outside the Church and to inspire them with confidence to finally proclaim, "This is the place."

> I pray that you, as covenant members of the Christ's Church, will lead out in this effort.

May we open our hearts to all of God's children.
May we repent of the patterns that drive them away.
May we endeavor together in the holy work of inclusion.
May we ever expand the borders of Zion.

ACKNOWLEDGMENTS

Expanding the Borders of Zion would not exist without the invaluable contributions of many supportive, talented individuals. Laurel Christensen Day provided experienced insight that gave me the confidence to take on this project. Tracy Keck edited the final manuscript, and no one in the world could have done a better job. The self-publishing process was new to me and proved challenging, but Brooke Romney offered firsthand advice, and Morgan and Bryan Crockett did a fantastic job typesetting and printing the book.

Many of my personal friends dedicated valuable time and effort to the content. Mitchell Poirier's spiritual insights inspired me to start writing and heavily influenced the first chapter you read. His creative contributions came full circle when he designed and drew the cover art. Molly Finlayson and Ben Schilaty provided help by acting as sounding boards and motivators toward the beginning of my writing process. As I further brought my ideas to life, Jared Fowkes was indispensable in helping me organize content and fill gaps in information. His personal experience, storytelling abilities, and passion for this subject proved incredibly impactful. He also helped me design the cover and created the official digital rendering.

My mom, Cathy Bird Wallace, also played an essential role. I relied heavily on her writing prowess for large portions of the initial manuscript. At one point in the writing process I felt overwhelmed and stuck, so I flew back to my hometown and spent an entire week writing with her. She dedicated countless hours to brainstorming, editing, and honing my words, and helped this this book become its very best version. I'm grateful for her efforts and proud to be her son.

Finally, Ryan Clifford deserves special acknowledgment. He has been my rock, my supporter, and my confidant since the earliest stages of this book. He grounds me in a way no one else can, and he helped me stay true to myself and to my message as I wrote. He provided practical feedback and drove me to "tell it like it is" by keeping the raw, uncomfortable portions of the book. His companionship and patience have been a lifeline for the past two years, and I'm grateful for his willingness to stand beside me. His character and dedication deserve praise and admiration. He's stepped into an incredibly uncomfortable space for me and has sacrificed more than should ever be expected. Ryan, I love you, and I feel so blessed to have you in my life. Thank you for staying and believing in me.

ABOUT THE AUTHOR

CHARLIE BIRD is an award-winning author, podcaster, therapist, and social media influencer based in Utah. He is known for performing as Cosmo the Cougar at Brigham Young University from 2016 to 2018, where he received national acclaim for his dance performances and viral mascot videos. Bird was born and raised in southwest Missouri and served a mission for The Church of Jesus Christ of Latter-day Saints in Redlands, California. He "bleeds blue," holding two undergraduate degrees from BYU, as well as a master's in social work. Charlie is passionate about bridging the gap between LGBTQ and religious communities, evident by his frequent work with nonprofit organizations and weekly involvement with the *Questions from the Closet* podcast. When he isn't writing, speaking, or advocating, Charlie can be found hiking the Wasatch mountains, traveling with friends, or tumbling at local gymnastics gyms. To stay up to date with all of Charlie's advocacy and adventures, you can find him on social media as @mrcharliebird.